JACK
of
FABLES

Turning Pages

BILL WILLINGHAM MATTHEW STURGES

Writers

RUSS BRAUN TONY AKINS

Pencillers

JOSÉ MARZÁN, JR. ANDREW PEPOY
STEVE LEIALOHA

Inkers

DANIEL VOZZO

Colorist

TODD KLEIN

Letterer

BRIAN BOLLAND *Original Series Covers*
JACK OF FABLES created by **BILL WILLINGHAM**

JACK *of* FABLES

Turning Pages

Cover illustration by Brian Bolland. Logo design by James Jean. Publication design by Brainchild Studios/NYC.

Table of Contents

Dramatis Personae

JACK
Also known as Little Jack Horner, Jack B. Nimble, Jack the Giant Killer and by countless other aliases, our hero Jack of the Tales embodies the archetype of the lovable rogue (minus, according to many, the lovability).

BIGBY WOLF
The biggest, baddest sheriff ever to wear the tin star, and one of Fabletown's staunchest defenders.

THE BOOKBURNER
The head librarian of Americana, and the Fables' worst nightmare.

KEVIN THORN
Newly revealed as the father of Mr. Revise and the son of the Pathetic Fallacy, he is currently a "guest" of the Golden Boughs.

GARY, THE PATHETIC FALLACY
A timid, impressionable and warm-hearted fellow whose power over inanimate objects is matched only by his love of Sousa marches.

HUMPTY DUMPTY
A stout fellow from Colchester, his ferocious bark belies his brittle nature.

MR. REVISE
Jack's untiring antagonist, dedicated to trapping Fables and draining their power in pursuit of a magic-free world.

RAVEN
Jack's new Native American companion, blessed with a contrary nature and some surprising abilities.

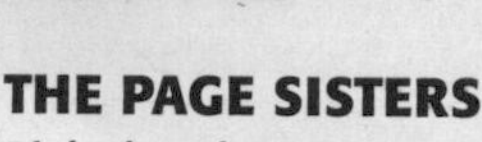

THE PAGE SISTERS
Right-hand women to Mr. Revise and the chief librarians at his Fable prison, the Golden Boughs Retirement Village.

Robin Page

Priscilla Page

Hillary Page

GOLDILOCKS
A self-styled revolutionary whose narcissism is almost equal to Jack's own.

LADY LUCK
A capricious tyrant, given to rhyming and brain-eating.

BABE
A blue ox with a gift for self-invention.

Looking back, anyone would have to admit that 1883 was a strange and wild year, and not by any definition a good one.
Fifty-three black folks were lynched in America.
WTS

Inspired by an American friend at an international arms show, who said, "If you wish to make a pile of money, invent something that will enable these Europeans to cut each other's throats with greater facility." Hiram S. Maxim invented the first fully automatic machine gun.

A German fellow by the name of Friedrich Nietzsche declared that God was dead in his radical pamphlet titled *Also Sprach Zarathustra.*

And the Jack Candle Gang of desperadoes ran roughshod over the Wild West, robbing, rustling, killing and reaving wherever they went.
1883
CHAPTER ONE:
The Legend of Smilin' Jack
STAND AND DELIVER!
YOU KILLED MY GUARD STONE DEAD! HE HAD A WIFE AND SON!

NO ONE ELSE NEEDS TO DIE, AS LONG AS NO ONE ELSE DOES ANYTHING FRISKY.
AND PROVIDING YOU THROW DOWN THAT STRONGBOX POST HASTE!

Indian Wally Broadhome was a half-breed killer of the most unruly sort. He used to be a member of the Apache tribal police in Arizona Territory.

SO GRAB THAT STRONGBOX, PARD, AND MAKE SURE YOU KEEP BOTH HANDS IN SIGHT WHILE DOING IT.

That ended abruptly when he got it in his head to rob the reservation's quarterly payroll and supplies allotment from the U.S. Department of Indian Affairs.
I'LL BE TAKING THAT GOLD, IF IT'S ALL THE SAME TO YOU FELLOWS.
Just over twenty-seven thousand in pure yellow gold.

He didn't get away with so much as a plugged centavo. He learned a lesson that day: another term for lone robber is "target practice."

Coldstream Angus McKee was another sort of killer entirely.
NO ONE MOVE, 'ER THIS WEE SCATTERGUN MAKE GHOSTS OF THE LOT.

He earned his fancy name serving in Britain's famous Coldstream Guards — as deadly a collection of corpse-makers as ever trod God's good soil.

Decorated veteran of the Crimean War, he was drummed out of the regiment (after taking thirty lashes) for striking an officer. The Guards regretted it ever since.
No, not because they were too severe.

It turns out they were too lenient. The officer never recovered from Angus' single blow, being quite clearly "touched in the head" from that day on.
And then three weeks later, the old boy simply dropped dead, right in the middle of parade.

The guards searched high and low for Angus to execute him for murder, but by that time he'd long since hightailed it for the New World.

The Jasper Kid claimed to come from Jasper, Indiana, but that was a lie.
THERE'D BETTER BE CASH A-PLENTY IN THIS BOX, OR I'LL BE SORE PEEVED TO BE CERTAIN.

He really hailed from nearby Huntingburg, but no one could fear and respect an hombre who called himself the Huntingburg Kid.
YOU'RE A BAD ONE, YOUNG MAN!
AND YOU'RE A DEAD ONE WHO JUST DON'T KNOW IT YET, OLD MAN.

He was pure wickedness from the cradle. He signed onto the Candle Gang to earn a reputation, while perfecting his murdering ways.

Which brings us to the leader of the gang, Smilin' Jack Candle his very own self.
LET'S WRAP THIS UP, BOYS. CAN'T YOU SEE THESE FINE FOLKS WANT TO BE ON THEIR WAY?
BE RUDE TO KEEP THEM ANY LONGER.

He came from somewhere out east and claimed to be a hero of the Confederacy during the War of Northern Aggression. And who knows? He may have been.

The bleeding South produced a lot of penniless heroes out of those terrible years.

He was a bit of a dandy and always had a smile and a tip of his hat for man or child, and most especially for the fair sex.
TOP OF THE DAY TO YOU.
AND TO YOU, SIR.

But one look at his cold, dead eyes revealed the merciless snake within.

There were all sorts of rumors about Jack Candle and his exploits since the close of the war, but his first confirmed mention in the papers was in the early days of 1883.
FOUR JACKS AGAIN? THAT SIMPLY AIN'T POSSIBLE!
YOU, SIR, ARE A CHEAT AND A LOW CUR!

On February 16th, on the very day the Ladies' Home Journal published its first issue, Jack gunned a man down in the Chisholm Creek saloon in Wichita, Kansas.
SMILE WHEN YOU SAY THAT, DUDE, SO I'LL KNOW WE'RE STILL FRIENDS.

He claimed it was a fair fight, but a jury of twelve good men and true saw it differently.
...SENTENCE YOU TO BE HANGED BY THE NECK UNTIL DEAD, TWO WEEKS FROM TODAY, AND MAY GOD HAVE MERCY ON YOUR SOUL.

On the morning of April 13th, the same day that the notorious Alfred Packer was convicted of cannibalism, Jack escaped the hangman, shooting his way free.

He shot seven men that day, two of whom eventually died of their wounds, including Wichita's town marshal.

No one knew how he got the guns.

But it should be noted the young widow Watersmith had visited him not twenty minutes earlier with a covered breakfast tray for his last meal.
I'LL ALWAYS LOVE YOU, JACK.
HOW COULD YOU NOT?

Smilin' Jack Candle was a wanted man from that day forward. Every newspaper in the Christian world carried the story.
THAT HAS TO BE JACK HORNER.
JACK CANDLE ESCAPES
DEADLY SHOOTOUT IN WICHITA CLAIMS
AND YOU'RE SURE HE'S ONE OF OURS? THIS JACK FELLOW IS A FABLE?

Jack got clean away, showing up again in Oklahoma Indian Territory, and this time he had a gang of fellow desperadoes.
KEEP YOUR HANDS CLEAR OF THOSE LEVERS, GENTLEMEN, OR I'LL HAVE TO BURN YOU DOWN.

It was the first of May, the same day the Amsterdam World's Fair opened and Buffalo Bill inaugurated his Wild West Show.
QUIT SHOOTING AT GOD, JASPER. HE DON'T LIKE IT.
YOU MAY NEED THOSE ROUNDS, KID, WHEN THEY SEND THE PINKERTONS AFTER US.

Then on May 27th, two events of note happened: Alexander the Third was crowned Czar of all Russia, and the Jack Candle Gang robbed the bank in the silver-mining boom town of Chloride, New Mexico.

Plenty of blood was spilled on both occasions.

The civilized world was outraged. Bounties piled up, but no one collected them.
I WANT JACK CANDLE HANGING FROM A NEW ROPE BEFORE ANOTHER MONTH PASSES!
THERE'LL BE NO OFFERS OF AMNESTY THIS TIME!
YES, GOVERNOR.
BEN HUR

But no posse ever caught up with the Candle Gang. Not even the legendary Pinkertons could pin them down.
THIS SIGN IS THREE DAYS OLD. MAYBE FOUR.

Then a stranger came from the east. He stepped down from the train in Albuquerque wearing a star on the vest of his greenhorn eastern suit.
ALBUQUERQUE
HERE, SON. I HAVE A HORSE IN THE LIVESTOCK CAR. GO FETCH HIM FOR ME.
WOW! A NICKEL ALL MY OWN?
AND ANOTHER NICKEL ON TOP OF THAT WHEN YOU FETCH MY BAGS AND SADDLE FROM THE TRAIN-- AND AFTER I'VE SEEN FOR MYSELF THAT YOU TREATED MY HORSE GENTLE.
CALL HIM TATE AND HE WON'T GIVE YOU NO TROUBLE.
THANKS, MISTER!

He claimed to be a sheriff from some-place back east, but never quite specified where.
GOOD EVENING, MARSHAL. WHAT'S THE LATEST REPORT ON THE JACK CANDLE GANG? I'VE BEEN TRAVELING TOO LONG TO BE CAUGHT UP ON THE NEWS.

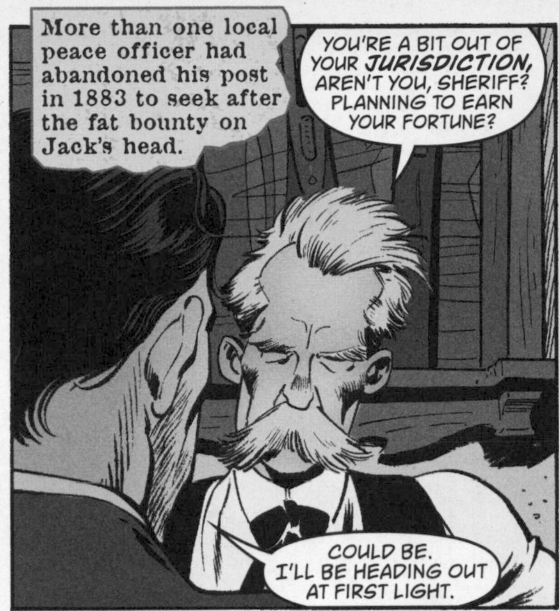
More than one local peace officer had abandoned his post in 1883 to seek after the fat bounty on Jack's head.
YOU'RE A BIT OUT OF YOUR JURISDICTION, AREN'T YOU, SHERIFF? PLANNING TO EARN YOUR FORTUNE?
COULD BE. I'LL BE HEADING OUT AT FIRST LIGHT.

He stayed only one night in the hotel, and was quite transformed in the morning.
RIDING OUT ALONE?
YEP.
DAMN FOOL THING TO DO, IF YOU ASK ME. BUT I GUESS A MAN HAS A GOD-GIVEN RIGHT TO BE STUPID.

HEY! I DON'T SEE YOU SPORTIN' ANY IRON!
NEVER HAD MUCH USE FOR FIREARMS.

WELL, I DIDN'T REALIZE IT'S SUICIDE YOU'RE AFTER. STEP DOWN, STRANGER. I'LL PLUG YOU MY OWN SELF AND SAVE YOU A HARD RIDE.
THANKS FOR THE KIND OFFER, MARSHAL, BUT I GUESS I'LL LET JACK HAVE FIRST TRY.

On the 30th of May, a rumor that the Brooklyn Bridge was about to collapse caused a stampede that killed twelve. The Candle Gang only killed three that day.
OW!

On the ninth day of June, the first commercial electric railway line began operation in Chicago and the Candle Gang robbed the Wells Fargo office in Tularosa.
GOT A BURR UNDER YOUR SADDLE, TATE?
NO, I'M JUST NOT USED TO HAVING A SADDLE IN THE FIRST PLACE, OR A RIDER IN IT FOR THAT MATTER. WHY WAS IT NECESSARY I COME ALONG ON THIS FOOL'S ERRAND, BIGBY?

By July 24th, the Arabi Pasha declared a holy war in far Egypt, and an unarmed sheriff named Bigby Wolf pursued a more private war in New Mexico.
YOU'D MAKE BETTER TIME AS A WOLF.
ICHABOD CRANE WOULDN'T LET ME COME OUT HERE UNLESS I PROMISED TO STAY HUMAN AS MUCH AS POSSIBLE. HE'S PERPETUALLY WORRIED THE MUNDYS WILL SCOPE OUT OUR SECRET.

He rode a white horse named Incitatus — Tate for short.
WELL, A GIANT WOLF WOULD STAND OUT--EVEN IN THIS DESOLATE LAND.
YEP. SO I NEED A HORSE, BECAUSE STALKING JACK ON FOOT WOULD BE TOO MUCH FOR ANY MUNDY TO SWALLOW.
IT'S BAD ENOUGH I DON'T GO HEELED.

AND SINCE, DUE TO MY WOLFISH NATURE, NO MUNDY HORSE WILL ABIDE ME ON ITS BACK, YOU WERE ELECTED TO COME WITH.
HAS TO BE A NICE CHANGE FROM BEING COOPED UP ON THE FARM.

MORE FOLKS TO TALK TO BACK HOME, THOUGH. WHEN DO YOU THINK WE MIGHT RUN ACROSS JACK'S TRAIL?
ALREADY DID. BEEN CLOSING IN ON HIM FOR TWO DAYS.

WHO IS IT, JACK?

I DON'T RIGHTLY KNOW. FELLA LOOKS A BIT *FAMILIAR*, BUT I CAN'T PLACE HIM.

WELL, WHOEVER HE BE, IT'S CLEAR HE'S HUNTING *US*. HE HASN'T DEVIATED FROM OUR TRAIL SINCE WE FIRST SET EYES ON HIM.
YES. HE'S A SKILLED *TRACKER*-- READING OUR SIGN WITHOUT EVER GETTING DOWN FROM THE SADDLE. NEVER SEEN THAT *DONE*.

NOT A SMART MAN, THOUGH, TO COME AT US ALL ON HIS *OWN*. LET'S RIDE DOWN THERE AND SHOOT HIM.
WHY? I CAN DROP HIM FROM UP *HERE* WITH MY LONG GUN.

BUT THEN I COULDN'T QUESTION HIM FIRST. THE *MAN'S* GOT ME CURIOUS.

On the very same day a volcano on the island of Ischia, Italy killed more than two thousand people. Jack Candle took a notion to gun down just one lone rider.
NOW REMEMBER, IF ANY OF YOU CLEARS LEATHER BEFORE I DO, I'LL PLUG YOU MYSELF.

HOWDY, STRANGER. DUSTY DAY, HUH?
AFTERNOON, JACK.

OH, SO YOU KNOW ME THEN? AND WHO MIGHT YOU BE?
WHAT BUSINESS MIGHT YOU HAVE WITH JACK CANDLE AND HIS FRIENDS?

I GOT NO BUSINESS AT ALL WITH JACK CANDLE. MY BUSINESS IS WITH JACK HORNER.

OH.
NOW I RECOGNIZE YOU.

NAME'S BILBY, RIGHT?
CLOSE ENOUGH. TIME TO COME HOME, JACK.

I DON'T THINK SO, PARD. BUT IF YOU TURN AROUND RIGHT NOW, I'LL THINK ABOUT LETTING YOU RIDE OUT OF HERE.
LOOK AT THIS IGNORANT TINHORN! HE'S GOT NO GUN! THINKS A TIN STAR IS ENOUGH TO PROTECT HIM!

I DON'T THINK SO, JACK. ONE WAY OR ANOTHER YOU'RE COMING IN.

SITTING UPRIGHT OR DRAPED OVER THE SADDLE. MAKES NO DIFFERENCE TO ME.
TOUGH WORDS, HOMBRE.

CRACK!
BLAM!
WELL, I TRIED TO REASON WITH YOU, SHERIFF.
BANG!
POW!
BURN HIM DOWN, BOYS! POUR LEAD INTO HIM!

KEEP SHOOTING!
EMPTY YOUR GUNS INTO HIM!

THEN RELOAD AND SHOOT HIM SOME MORE!
IF YOU SAY, BUT I PROFFER HE'S FULL DEAD BY NOW.
JUST DO AS I SAY!
BLAM! BLAM! CRACK! BLAM! POWW! BLAM!

GOOD ENOUGH!
NOW LET'S RIDE!
WHERE YOU OFF TO, WALLY?
AFTER THE MAN'S HORSE. IT RAN OFF THAT WAY.

NEXT: NIGHT OF THE WOLF

WE HERE AT FABLES CENTRAL REALIZE YOU'VE JUST ENDURED THE FIRST ISSUE OF JACK OF FABLES WITHOUT A SINGLE INTENTIONAL FUNNY BIT. IN ORDER TO INCLUDE THE MINIMUM RECOMMENDED DAILY ALLOWANCE OF ***HOO-HAH,*** AND TO KEEP YOUR FUNNYBONE ***PROPERLY*** TICKLED UNTIL THIS SERIES GETS SILLY AGAIN, WE OFFER YOU THIS MODERN-DAY INTERLUDE WITH OUR FAVORITE MINIATURE BLUE OX:

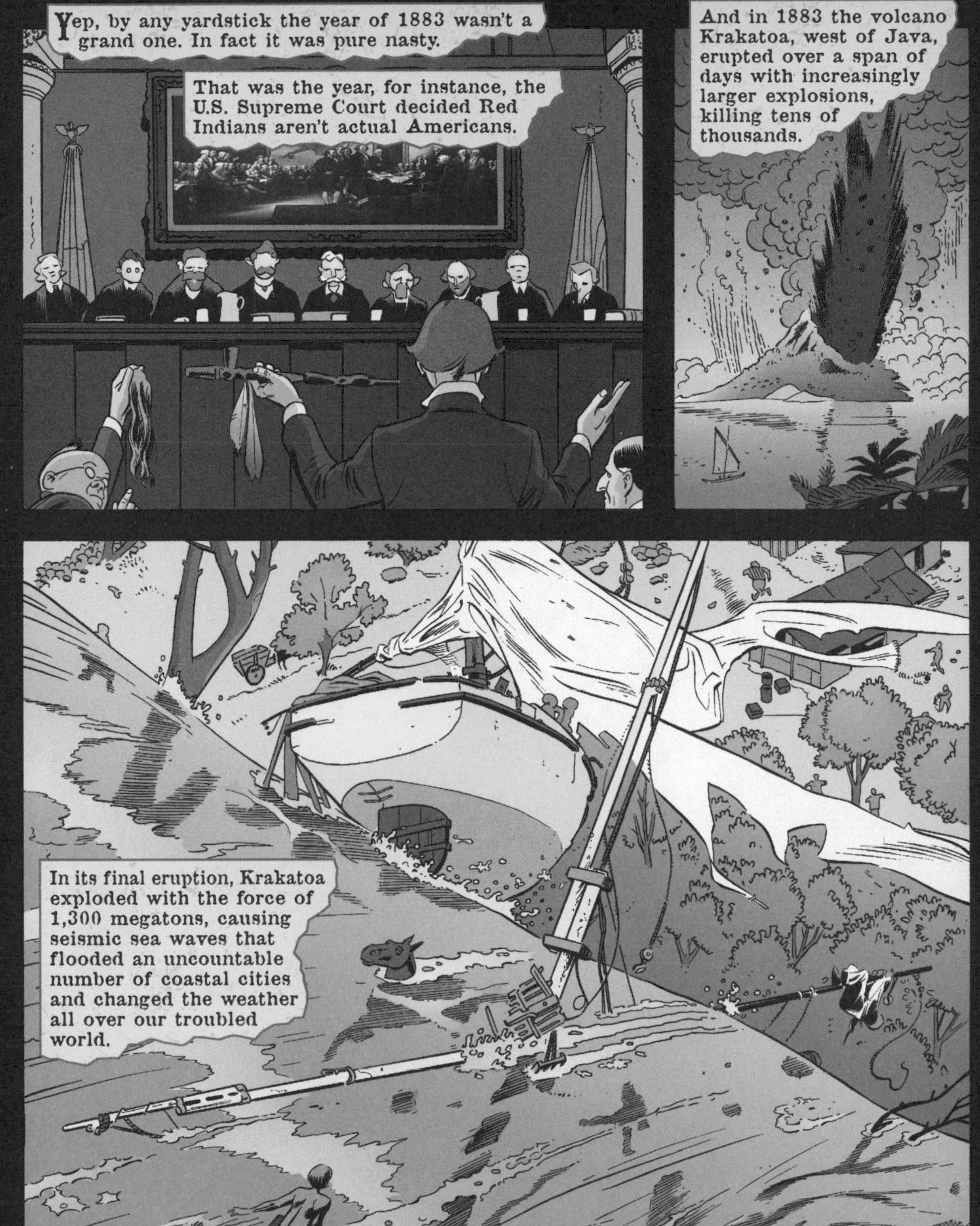

1883

CHAPTER TWO: MOON of the WOLF

On the first day of August the Inland Postal Service began in Great Britain, while the Jack Candle Gang spent their third day lying low in the New Mexico town of Lilly of the Valley.
WHAT'S THE MATTER, SWEETIE?
DON'T YOU LIKE ME NO MORE?
GRAND PALACE HOTEL

ORIENTAL PEARL SALOON
ANK

AW, IT'S NOT THAT, CLARA BELLE, I'M JUST SORE DISTRACTED IS ALL, AND THAT'S AFFECTED MY MOOD FOR LIFE'S EARTHLY PLEASURES.
BUT YOU'RE ALWAYS IN THE MOOD.

OLD MISTER HAWMAKER'S PRIZE BULL IS LESS RUT CRAZY THAN YOU.
HAWMAKER'S BULL DOESN'T HAVE A BIG BAD WOLF ON HIS MIND.

HUH?
NEVER YOU MIND, CLARA DARLIN'. HAND ME MY PANTS. I NEED TO GO SEE IF MORGANSTERNIN HAS MY SPECIAL ORDER READY.

GUNSMITH
S. MORGANSTERNIN PROPRIETOR
FORGIVE ME PLEASE, MISTER CANDLE, SIR!
BUT I TOLD YOU IT WOULD TAKE MORE TIME TO COMPLETE AN UNUSUAL ORDER SUCH AS YOU REQUIRE.

BUT ONLY YESTERDAY YOU SAID YOU HAD THEM NEARLY DONE-- A BOX OF FIFTY NEW CARTRIDGES FOR MY SIX-SHOOTER, THE BULLETS MADE OF PUREST SILVER.
AND I DID, MISTER CANDLE, SIR. I COMPLETED THEM, ONLY--

ONLY WHAT?
ONLY SOME MYSTERIOUS MASKED FELLER CAME IN AND PURCHASED THE WHOLE LOT EARLY THIS MORNING.

STRANGE DUDE HE WAS. HE HAD AN INDIAN SIDEKICK AND--

YOU SOLD MY SILVER BULLETS TO SOMEONE ELSE?
WELL, MASKED AS HE WAS, I NATURALLY ASSUMED HE WAS PART OF YOUR GANG--UHM, THAT IS TO SAY, YOUR BUSINESS ASSOCIATES.

BUT WHEN HE SAID HE WAS HEADED UP MONTANA WAY, I CONSIDERED MAYBE I'D MADE A MISTAKE AND ASKED FOR THE ROUNDS BACK, BUT HE SAID A DEAL'S A DEAL AND--

AND YOU ALREADY HAD HIS MONEY IN YOUR POCKET.

IF YOU'LL JUST BE PATIENT FOR ANOTHER THREE OR FOUR MORE DAYS, I CAN REPLACE YOUR ORDER.
I DON'T HAVE THREE OR FOUR MORE DAYS! I'VE STAYED HERE IN THE SAME TOWN TOO LONG ALREADY!

BIGBY WILL BE BACK ON MY TRAIL BY NOW!
AND BECAUSE OF YOUR GREED AND PURE INCOMPETENCE, I STILL GOT NO WAY TO KILL HIM PERMANENT DEAD!
BLAM!

EEEHH

WAS THAT GUNFIRE I HEARD, MISTER CANDLE, SIR?
OF COURSE IT WAS, WICKERSTEIN. I WAS IN A GUNSMITH'S SHOP, WASN'T I? NEEDED TO SEE IF MY SIX-SHOOTER STILL SHOOTS TRUE, DIDN'T I?

TURNS OUT IT DOES.
OH, BY THE WAY, SHERIFF, OLD MAN MORGANSTERNIN IS DEAD INSIDE. I BELIEVE YOU'LL FIND HE DIED OF NATURAL GRIEF OVER THE REALIZATION OF A LIFE MISSPENT.
OH, DEAR.

BUT BEFORE YOU DEAL WITH THAT, GO DRAG MY TWO PARTNERS OUT OF WHATEVER SALOON OR FANCY HOUSE THEY'RE CURRENTLY PASSED OUT IN.

TELL THEM TO GET READY FOR A HARD RIDE.
HO
YES SIR, MISTER CANDLE!

Elsewhere...
DID THE BLOOD COME OUT?

MOST OF IT.
NOTHING I CAN DO ABOUT THE BULLET HOLES, THOUGH.

YOU SHOULD'VE PACKED ANOTHER SHIRT.
SHOULD'VE DONE A LOT OF THINGS DIFFERENT. NO USE CRYING ABOUT IT NOW.

I'M ONLY SAYING THAT IF YOU RIDE INTO A TOWN WEARING A SHIRT RIDDLED WITH BULLET HOLES, BUT NO ACTUAL WOUNDS UNDERNEATH, PEOPLE ARE APT TO GET CURIOUS.
JUST THE SORT OF CONUNDRUM ICHABOD ORDERED US TO AVOID.

I DOUBT ANY MUNDY WILL SEE ME IN THIS SHIRT AND IMMEDIATELY LEAP TO THE NOTION THAT I MUST BE A MAGICAL WEREWOLF FROM A SECRET SOCIETY OF EQUALLY MAGICAL FOLKS BACK EAST.
GRANTED, IT'S NOT LIKELY, BUT I'M JUST SAYING...

YOU'RE JUST SAYING TOO MUCH, TATE. A TALKING HORSE WOULD BE A LOT HARDER TO EXPLAIN THAN A RUINED SHIRT.
WHO'S GOING TO OVERHEAR ME OUT HERE?

ME FOR ONE. I'M TIRED OF LISTENING TO YOU WHINE AND MOAN. I'D LIKE A LITTLE PEACEFUL QUIET FOR A TIME.
SURE THING, BIGBY. YOU DON'T NEED TO TELL ME TWICE. I LIKE TO PASS A QUIET AFTERNOON AS MUCH AS THE NEXT FABLE.

I CAN BE AS QUIET AS A CHURCH MOUSE WHEN NEED BE-- AND NOT A CHURCH MOUSE LIKE LITTLE PIPPIN PEPPER UP AT THE FARM NEITHER.
LORD ABOVE BUT THAT CHILD CAN CHATTER ON AND ON. I DON'T KNOW WHERE IT COMES FROM.

SERIOUSLY. SHUT UP NOW.

SAY NO MORE, BIGBY. I CAN TAKE A HINT. YOU WON'T HEAR ANOTHER PEEP FROM ME.

AFTER ALL, YOU'RE THE BOSS OF THIS EXPEDITION. YOU WANT TALK AND WE'LL TALK. YOU WANT QUIET AND MUM'S THE WORD.
NO ONE NEEDS TO TELL ME TWICE.

Less than twenty miles distant...
WHERE'RE WE OFF TO SO FAST, JACK?

MONTANA.
WHAT FOR?
TWO REASONS.

FIRST, IT'S A LONG WAY AWAY FROM HERE, AND THIS TERRITORY AIN'T SAFE NO MORE.
SECOND, SOME HOMBRE HEADED TO MONTANA HAS SOMETHING OF MINE, AND I AIM TO GET IT BACK.

AND THIRD, BECAUSE I SAID SO.
NOW, SINCE ONE OF THE BENEFITS OF BEING BOSS IS NOT NEEDING TO EXPLAIN YOURSELF TO UNDERLINGS, I'LL THANK YOU TO CHOOSE ANOTHER SUBJECT TO JAW ABOUT.

Back at Lilly of the Valley...

...AND THEN THE OTHER BILLY GOAT GRUFF SAYS TO ME, HE **SAYS,** "I KILLED MANY A BRIDGE TROLL, ALL MUCH BIGGER THAN **YOU,** SO NO UPPITY PLOW HORSE WON'T GIVE ME NO TROUBLE."

AND SO I SAYS BACK TO **HIM,** I SAYS, "I AIN'T NO PLOW HORSE, BILL. I WAS A **SENATOR** OF ROME ONCE AND NEVER NO LOWLY--"

OKAY, TATE, NOW YOU **HAVE** TO BE QUIET.

YOU DON'T WANT T'BE ASKING QUESTIONS ABOUT JACK CANDLE AROUND HERE, MISTER.
SOME HERE LIKE HIM AND OTHERS ARE SO SCARED OF HIM THAT IT STILL ADDS UP TO THE SAME. SMILIN' JACK FAIRLY OWNS THIS TOWN.
CURIOUS.

I'VE GOT THREE LADIES, WHICH I EXPECT ARE GOOD ENOUGH TO TAKE THE POT.
BEATS MY TWO PAIR.

ONE MOMENT OF YOUR TIME, STRANGER.
I HEAR TELL YOU'VE BEEN ASKING A LOT OF NOSEY QUESTIONS ABOUT A FRIEND OF OURS.
MOVE YOUR HAND, BOY. I'M NOT ACCUSTOMED TO BEING PAWED AT.

IF YOU'RE FEELING INTRUDED UPON, SETTLE IT LIKE A MAN. STAND UP AND DRAW IRON.
I'M NOT WEARING A GUN.

NOT WEARING MUCH ELSE, EITHER--EXCEPT RAGS. LOOK AT THAT SHIRT.

RAGS INDEED. AND HE SMELLS LIKE NEW HORSE APPLES IN AN UNCLEANED BARN.

SAVE YOUR LIVES, BOYS. WALK AWAY NOW.

WHO CAN WALK AWAY WHEN YOU'VE BEEN JAWING ABOUT MY DEAREST FRIEND?
I WAS PRIVILEGED TO SERVE WITH COLONEL JACK CANDLE IN THE WAR, AMONG THE TEXAS VOLUNTEERS.

ODD, SINCE JACK NEVER ROSE ABOVE THE RANK OF CAPTAIN AND WAS WITH THE LOUISIANA VOLUNTEERS.
YOU CALLIN' ME A LIAR?

I'M NOT CALLING YOU ANYTHING, EXCEPT A MAN WHO'S BEGGING TO FILL A GRAVE.

YOU SHOULD'VE MOVED YOUR HAND WHEN YOU STILL HAD A CHANCE TO KEEP IT.

FIGHT! FIGHT!
ABOUT DAMN TIME!

SINCE JACK RODE OUT, THIS TOWN'S BEEN GRIEVOUSLY TOO CALM FOR MY TASTE!

GOOD TIME TO SETTLE SOME SCORES!
YOU BEEN SPARKIN' MY BEST SWEETHEART, LARRY BROGAN! I KNOWS IT!

On the fifth of August, in 1883, such a brawl broke out in the town of Lilly of the Valley, New Mexico, that it made most of the territory's papers.
LUCKY STRIKE SALOON

Two men were killed outright. Three more later died of their injuries, and half a dozen others were maimed for life.
MY HAND'S GONE!

At the same time Smilin' Jack and his two surviving cohorts were nearly three hundred miles to the north and hadn't so much as cleared leather in four days.
MY POOR HAND!
SOMEONE RIPPED IT CLEAN OFF!

This was one calamity that couldn't be blamed on the Candle Gang. Some reports had it that a stranger from back East started all the ruckus.

Riding hard and fast, barely stopping to camp at night, the Candle Gang made it to the sprawling ranch lands around Laramie, Wyoming by mid August.

YEAH, THE MASKED MAN CAME THROUGH HERE ALL RIGHT.

WITH ONLY THE HELP OF HIS FAITHFUL COMPANION, HE CAUGHT A WHOLE PASSEL OF RUSTLERS, RESTORED MY HERDS, RECOVERED MY MONEY **AND** SAVED MY RANCH FROM THE EVIL BANKERS BEHIND IT ALL.

YOUR TWENTY DAYS ARE UP, STRANGER. YOU'RE FREE TO GO.
JAIL

BUT TAKE HEED: CAUSE ANY MORE **TROUBLE** AND I'LL HAVE TO ARREST YOU AGAIN.
FIND ANY MORE TROUBLE, YOU MEAN--TROUBLE OTHERS STARTED.

JUDGE KRATER SAW IT DIFFERENT.
THE SAME JUDGE BOUGHT AND PAID FOR BY **JACK,** JUST LIKE THE LOCAL SHERIFF? I SEEM TO RECALL HE WAS DRUNK AND PASSED OUT IN THE CORNER ALL THROUGH THE FIGHT.
WANTED

NOW, HOLD ON! THAT SORT OF SLANDEROUS **GOSSIP** ISN'T CALLED FOR!
THAT'S THE SORT OF LOOSE TALK THAT COULD GET A FELLER THROWN **BACK** IN JAIL-- OR WORSE.

LET'S GET SOMETHING STRAIGHT, SHERIFF. YOU DIDN'T THROW **ME** IN JAIL--I WENT WILLINGLY.
I'M UNDER STRICT **ORDERS** TO ACT NICELY AMONG THE WEAK SCUM AND LOW CURS WHO INHABIT THESE LANDS.

BUT THE GENTLE SIDE OF MY NATURE IS THIN AND EASILY THWARTED BY THE BAD MANNERS OF IMBECILES, CORRUPT BUREAUCRATS AND OTHER SPECIES OF COWARD.

TAKE CARE, LEST I COME BACK HERE TO CLEAN UP THIS BLIGHTED TOWN ONCE I'VE CONCLUDED MY BUSINESS WITH JACK.
UNDERSTOOD, SIR.

I SHOULD BE GONE TWO OR THREE WEEKS AT THE MOST, AND I WANT YOU TO LOOK AFTER MY HORSE WHILE I'M AWAY.
LILLY LIVERY AND STABLE

HERE. THIS SHOULD COVER IT. IF I HAVE ANY CHANGE COMING, WE CAN SETTLE UP WHEN I RETURN.
FAIR ENOUGH, STRANGER.
NOW, WHY DON'T YOU GO BUY YOURSELF LUNCH WHILE I SAY GOODBYE TO MY HORSE? I LIKE A BIT OF PRIVACY IN MY MOMENTS OF SENTIMENT TOWARDS DUMB ANIMALS.

I'M MORE THAN TWENTY DAYS BEHIND JACK NOW AND I NEED TO MOVE *FAST*, SO YOU'LL HAVE TO STAY HERE AND SUFFER UNDER DAILY BRUSHING AND GOOD FEED.

I GUESS I CAN PUT UP WITH THAT FOR A WEEK OR TWO.

JUST MAKE SURE YOU REMEMBER YOU'RE A MUNDY HORSE NOW. ABSOLUTELY *NO* TALKING.
OF COURSE, BIGBY. WHAT KIND OF AN *IDIOT* DO YOU THINK I AM? NO ONE WILL HEAR A PEEP OUT OF ME. NO NEED TO TELL ME TWICE. MUM IS *DEFINITELY* THE WORD.

On the 8th of September in 1883 the famous golden spike was driven into the rails at Independence Creek, Montana, uniting the nation with the first continent-wide railroad.

The very next day that same solid gold spike was pried out of the rails and stolen by the Jack Candle Gang, who sent letters bragging about their deed to more than a dozen national papers. Four guards were slain in the dirty deed.
On the same night many residents of northern Wyoming and southern Montana reported seeing a giant demon wolf running north under the light of a full moon.
NEXT: THE SHOWDOWN!

A SECOND ISSUE OF JACK OF FABLES HAS NOW COME AND GONE WITHOUT A SINGLE INTENTIONALLY FUNNY MOMENT? ARE WE GETTING TIRESOME AND SERIOUS IN OUR OLD AGE? ARE WE "MELLOWING OUT," AS THEY SAY? NOPE--AND HERE'S A RIDICULOUS BABE PAGE TO PROVE IT...

CHAPTER THREE: The SHOWDOWN

But also throughout the year of 1883, the dirty little coward Robert Ford assassinated Jesse James time and again, often two or three times a day.
He did it on a Broadway stage in New York City, reenacting for a usually packed house the vile deed he'd perpetrated in actuality the year before.
By his own estimation Bob Ford later opined that he must have backshot poor Jesse more than 800 times before he was finally booed off the stage forever.
MAKE FOR THE HORSES, BOYS!
WE'RE MOVIN' ON!
I CALCULATE THIS HIDEOUT'S PLUM USED UP ALL ITS UTILITY!
ABOUT DAMN TIME!
MONTANA'S FROSTIER THAN M'AULD HIGHLANDS, 'N THAS FER BLOODY DAMN SURE!

STUPID LAW DOGS!
DON'T YOU KNOW THAT WHEN YOU BRING MORE MEN IT JUST MEANS MORE *TARGETS* FOR ME TO GUN DOWN?
LOOKIE THERE! I JUST MADE SOMEONE A WIDOW!
And on the fourth day of October, the very same day that the Orient Express made its first run, linking Istanbul to Paris by rail, a small army of Pinkertons and local lawmen trapped the Jack Candle Gang in a log shack in the forest wilderness due west of Red Lodge Montana.
Amazingly, Jack and his two surviving companions boldly shot their way clear, killing seven good souls in the process.

Willem Van Buskirk, one of the surviving Pinkertons (who later served in President Cleveland's administration), went to his grave swearing that he'd managed to wound Jack Candle in that deadly shootout.
AND THERE! ANOTHER *WIDOW* MADE!

But most scholars agree that it was actually Coldstream Angus McKee who was wounded that day.
RYUP!

And it was never fully determined that Van Buskirk scored the hit.
I FEAR ONE OF THE LADS GOT OFF A *LUCKY* ONE, JACK!
I'M SHOT PURE!

What historians do agree upon is that all three members of the Candle Gang got away that day.
HOLD UP, JACK!
THIS WOUND IN M' BACK IS A BAD ONE. I CANNA RIDE FAST WITHOUT BLEEDING M'SELF EMPTY!

BAD LUCK, ANGUS, BUT THE LAW WILL BE NIPPING AT OUR HEELS IN NO TIME.
WE NEED TO KEEP RIDING HARD, OR WE'LL ALL HAVE HOLES IN OUR BACKS.

SPLIT OFF FROM US AND RIDE AS FAST AS YOU'RE ABLE TO. ANY POSSE IS LIKELY TO FOLLOW THE TRAIL WITH THE MOST HORSES.
JASPER AND I WILL TRY TO LEAD THEM AWAY FROM YOU.

IF YOU GET AWAY, MEET US BACK IN LILLY OF THE VALLEY.
I'VE GOT A TARDY NOTION WE WERE SAFER THERE ALL ALONG, WITH A WHOLE TOWN TO GUARD US.

NO SIGN OF RIDERS IN FOUR HOURS. GOOD NEWS. I THINK WE LOST 'EM.
WALK GENTLY, PONY. NO NEED TO HURRY NOW.
STILL--NO SENSE TEMPTING FATE BY LIGHTING A FIRE.
WE'LL HAVE A COLD CAMP TONIGHT.
AAAAAAAOOOOOOOOOO!
SETTLE DOWN, YE DAFT NAG! IT'S JUST A WOLF IN THE DISTANCE, HOWLING ITS LUST FOR THE LADIES OF ITS KIND!
NO WOLF WILL ENTER OUR CAMP, EVEN A DARK ONE. THEY'VE LEARNED WELL TO FEAR MAN AND HIS FIRE STICKS.
THE BOLDER ONES HAVE ALL BEEN WEEDED OUT BY NOW.

MAYBE SO!

BUT I'M NO TIMID MUNDY WOLF!

YEEEARRRGH!
YER A DEMON O' TH' NIGHT!
QUIT YOUR BLUBBERING, BOY. YOU DON'T HAVE THE TIME TO WASTE. YOU'RE DYING.

TRY TO GO OUT LIKE A MAN.

NO! I'VE SEEN MEN SURVIVE WORSE IN THE WAR! YOU CAN SAVE ME, IF YE WANT! I DON'T NEED TO DIE!
AND BE A LIVING WITNESS TO THE FACT OF A GIANT TALKING WOLF? NO, YOU'RE DONE FOR. ACCEPT IT.
BUT IF YOU TELL ME WHERE JACK IS, I'LL TAKE THE PAIN AWAY.

On the 13th of November, a poorly trained Egyptian army, led by the British General William Hicks, marched towards the El Obeid in the Sudan — straight into a Mahdist ambush.
NO, YOU MISS MY POINT, JACK. I WASN'T CRITICIZING YOUR GUNPLAY. BUT IN THAT SHOOTOUT AT THE MONTANA SHACK, YOU HAD A SIX-GUN, JUST LIKE THE TWO OF MINE.

Hicks and his entire command were massacred.
BUT TWICE IN A ROW YOU FIRED ONLY FIVE SHOTS BEFORE RELOADING. I'M JUST CURIOUS. WHY?

WELL, IT MIGHT BE THAT IT'S NONE OF YOUR BUSINESS. OR IT MIGHT BE THAT I'VE GOT A LUCKY BULLET IN THE SIXTH SLOT, WHICH I'M SAVING FOR A PARTICULAR MAN'S BELLY.

On the same day, Jack Candle and the Jasper Kid rode back into Lilly of the Valley for the last time.
NOW, JASPER, IS THAT THE EXTENT OF YOUR CURIOSITY, OR DO YOU ALSO HAVE QUESTIONS ABOUT HOW OFTEN I CHANGE MY SOCKS?
WELL, SINCE YOU ASKED, THE GANG'S DOWN TO JUST THE TWO OF US. THAT AIN'T NO PROPER OUTLAW GANG. IT'S A DUO.

Coldstream Angus McKee wasn't with them, nor was he ever seen again.
WE GOIN' TO RECRUIT ANY NEW GUNS WHILE WE'RE HERE?
NOPE. THE GANG IS DONE. TIME TO MOVE ON TO A NEW WALK OF LIFE.
MEANTIME, YOU CHECK US INTO THE HOTEL, WHILE I HAVE A JAW WITH THE SHERIFF.
HOTEL

HE NEVER WOULD SAY HIS NAME, JACK, BUT CLAIMED TO BE A SHERIFF FROM SOME JURISDICTION OUT EAST.
JAIL

HE WAS A SCARY FELLER, I TELL YOU. HE SAID HE ONLY LET ME ARREST HIM BECAUSE HE DIDN'T FEEL LIKE *KILLING* NO FELLOW LAWMAN, EVEN A BAD ONE CLEARLY IN JACK'S POCKET.
THAT HAD TO BE BIGBY, ALL RIGHT.

BUT YOU SAY HE LEFT TOWN?
YEAH, BUT DAMNED IF I KNOW *HOW,* SINCE HE DIDN'T TAKE THE STAGE AND HIS HORSE IS STILL IN OLD MAN HOFFEN-STEADER'S LIVERY.

REALLY?

I'VE JUST THOUGHT OF A CUNNING PLAN, WICKERSTEIN.
GO TELL JENNY BELLE THAT I EXPECT TO FIND HER IN MY *BED* IN TWENTY MINUTES' TIME. I'M SUDDENLY IN THE MOOD FOR ALL *SORTS* OF WORLDLY DELIGHTS.

I'M AFEARED JENNY FINALLY SUCCUMBED TO THE POX WHILST YOU WERE GONE, JACK. IT WAS A REAL NICE FUNERAL THOUGH, AND EVERYONE--
LILLY LIVERY AND STABLE

THEN FETCH CLARA BELLE, OR BIG FANNY, OR BARBARA THE DEUCE. FOR CHRIST'S SAKE, WICKERSTEIN, DON'T YOU GOT NO INITIATIVE? DO I HAVE TO THINK OF EVERYTHING?
AND STABLE

I SWEAR I'M DOOMED TO BE PERPETUALLY ENCUMBERED BY IDJITS OF ALL STRIPES.

CLEAR OUT, HOFFENSTEADER. I GOTS BUSINESS ALONE AMONG THESE FLEA-BITTEN NAGS.
Y-Y-YES, SIR, MR. CANDLE, SIR.

NOW, LET'S SEE...LET'S SEE... LET'S SEE...
WHICH ONE OF YOU DID I SEE BIGBY RIDING BACK WHEN?

COULD IT BE--
YOU?
OH NO, SIR. I'M JUST A SIMPLE MUNDY HORSE. I THINK YOU WANT THAT SHIFTY-LOOKING SORREL IN THE NEXT STALL.

OH, I SEE. AND WILL THAT SORREL BE AS WELL SPOKEN AS YOU?
RATS!
LISTEN, YOU CAN'T KILL ME, JACK. I'M A LEGALLY DEPUTIZED OFFICER OF THE LAW. AND NOT ONLY THAT, I WAS A SENATOR OF ROME ONCE.

WHAT'S YOUR NAME, SON?
INCITATUS.
TATE, FOR SHORT.
WELL, HERE'S WHAT YOU'RE GOING TO DO, TATE.

YOU'RE GOING TO RIDE OUT AND FIND YOUR BOSS, AND YOU'RE GOING TO TELL HIM THAT HIS JOB'S ALL DONE AND THE TWO OF YOU CAN HEAD BACK TO FABLETOWN.
I HAVE RETIRED FROM THE OUTLAW TRADE AND DECIDED TO MOVE ON, TO EUROPE, OR AFRICA, OR THE FAR JAPANS, OR SOME-PLACE EQUALLY EXOTIC.

YOU MAKE HIM LISTEN TO YOU, TATE, OR SO HELP ME, I WILL HUNT YOU DOWN AND PLUG YOU STONE DEAD!
AND TELL HIM, IF HE DOESN'T GO AWAY, I GOT A DEADLY SURPRISE IN STORE FOR HIM!

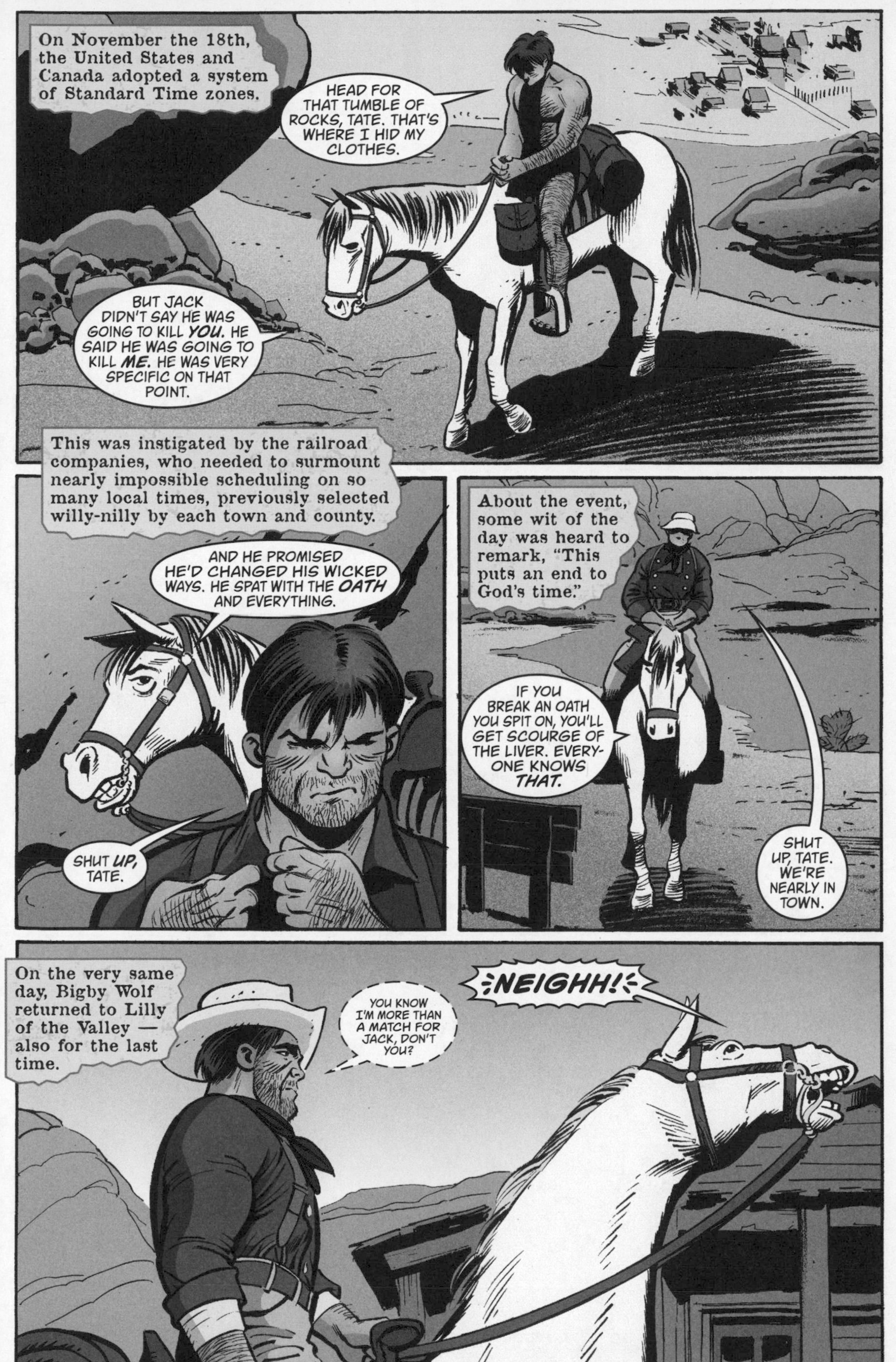
On November the 18th, the United States and Canada adopted a system of Standard Time zones.
HEAD FOR THAT TUMBLE OF ROCKS, TATE. THAT'S WHERE I HID MY CLOTHES.
BUT JACK DIDN'T SAY HE WAS GOING TO KILL YOU. HE SAID HE WAS GOING TO KILL ME. HE WAS VERY SPECIFIC ON THAT POINT.
This was instigated by the railroad companies, who needed to surmount nearly impossible scheduling on so many local times, previously selected willy-nilly by each town and county.
AND HE PROMISED HE'D CHANGED HIS WICKED WAYS. HE SPAT WITH THE OATH AND EVERYTHING.
SHUT UP, TATE.
About the event, some wit of the day was heard to remark, "This puts an end to God's time."
IF YOU BREAK AN OATH YOU SPIT ON, YOU'LL GET SCOURGE OF THE LIVER. EVERY-ONE KNOWS THAT.
SHUT UP, TATE. WE'RE NEARLY IN TOWN.
On the very same day, Bigby Wolf returned to Lilly of the Valley — also for the last time.
YOU KNOW I'M MORE THAN A MATCH FOR JACK, DON'T YOU?
NEIGHH!

The sheriff from back East let the boy live, remarking to all there to hear it that he wasn't interested in arresting no one but Jack.

LOOK WHAT THE MAN DID, JACK! HE BIT BOTH TRIGGER FINGERS CLEAN OFF!

AND I DIDN'T SEE HIM NEVER SPIT THEM OUT NONE, EITHER!

WAIT! WHERE ARE YOU GOING? AREN'T YOU GOING TO STAND WITH ME?
JUST LIKE YOU STOOD WITH ANGUS OR INDIAN WALLY? THAT SORT OF LOYALTY?
NO, JACK, YOU SAID THE GANG WAS DONE, AND I'M TAKING YOU AT YOUR WORD.

Less than a year later, a man calling himself Martin Rameau Tyler began making a name for himself in Southern California by investing in citrus orchards.
I QUIT, FORTHWITH, NOW AND IMMEDIATELY.
I GOT MOST OF MY POKE FROM ALL OUR JOBS STILL SAVED UP. I'M GOING TO FIND SOMEWHERE TO SPEND IT.

Mr. Tyler was notable both for his young age and the fact that he was missing a finger from each hand.
BUT WHAT ABOUT ME? WHERE'S THE TOWNFOLK? HOW COME THEY AREN'T ALL TAKING TO THE STREET TO PROTECT ME?

Tyler later invested his citrus fortune to help start the fledgling moving picture industry and became a Hollywood tycoon.
COME OUT, JACK, AND FACE YOUR FATE LIKE A MAN!
THIS DON'T INVOLVE THE TOWN! IT'S JUST ME AND YOU NOW!

Only on his deathbed in 1944 did Tyler claim to have once been the infamous Jasper Kid.
DON'T MAKE ME COME DRAG YOU OUT HERE!

OKAY, BIGBY, I'M COMING OUT, BUT I ALREADY SAID I WASN'T NO OUTLAW NO MORE. I'VE CHANGED ALL MY CRIMINAL WAYS.
SO WE REALLY GOT NO FURTHER BUSINESS TOGETHER.
YOU CAN GO BACK TO NEW YORK AND I'LL GO SOMEWHERE THE WHOLE OTHER SIDE OF THE WORLD AWAY, AND WE WON'T EVER NEED TO QUARREL WITH EACH OTHER FOR--

HEY!

YOU AIN'T PACKIN' IRON.

SO WHAT? IF I EVER NEED A GUN TO GET THE DROP ON A SHIFTLESS YAHOO LIKE YOU, I'LL GIVE UP POLICING FOREVER.

YOU MAY THINK SO, MISTER SCARY WOLF, BUT YOU DON'T REALIZE WHAT I GOT LOADED THIS TIME.
A SILVER BULLET, THAT'S WHAT! HOW 'BOUT THAT, HUH? BETCHA DIDN'T EXPECT THAT.

JUST ONE?

WELL, I--
THEN USE IT, IF YOU GOT IT. LET'S SEE IF YOU CAN CLEAR LEATHER AND BURN ME DOWN BEFORE I CAN CROSS THE DISTANCE BETWEEN US AND RIP YOUR THROAT OUT.

NOW, HOLD IT RIGHT THERE! I'M SERIOUS! I REALLY GOT A SILVER ROUND THAT CAN KILL YOU FULL DEAD, RIGHT WHERE YOU STAND.
THEN YOU GOT ME DEAD TO RIGHTS. BUT WHY'S YOUR HAND SHAKING?

HOLD IT, BIGBY, OR I'LL--
TALKING'S OVER!

COMMENCE TO FIGHTING!

THAT'S ENOUGH! THAT'S ALL!
I GIVE UP! I SURRENDER!
DON'T HIT ME NO MORE!
WHY DID YOU EVEN COME AFTER ME, BIGBY? I DIDN'T DO NOTHING AGAINST FABLETOWN! WHAT DID I EVER DO TO YOU?
WHAT DID YOU DO?
WHAT DID YOU DO?
YOU ROBBED AND LOOTED AND YOU KILLED FOLKS, JACK!
YOU GUNNED THEM DOWN BY THE DOZENS, WITHOUT A SECOND THOUGHT!

SO WHAT?
THEY WEREN'T REAL PEOPLE--NOT FABLES!

LOOK AT THEM! THEY'RE JUST WORTHLESS MUNDYS!
THEY DON'T COUNT!
THEY DON'T LIVE LONG ENOUGH TO COUNT FOR NOTHING!

AND THEY KNOW IT, TOO! LOOK AT THE WAY THEY KILL EACH OTHER! I SAW IT IN THE WAR!
THEY DON'T CARE NOTHING ABOUT KILLING EACH OTHER BY THE THOUSANDS, ALL IN A SINGLE AFTERNOON! I SAW IT EVERY DAY IN THE WAR!

KILLING MUNDYS AIN'T NO CRIME ANY MORE THAN STOMPING ON BUGS! HOW CAN IT BE?
I FOUGHT IN THE WAR, TOO. AND IF THAT'S THE ONLY LESSON YOU TOOK FROM IT THEN YOU DIDN'T LEARN A DAMNED THING.

PACK YOUR THINGS, JACK. WE'LL BE RIDING OUT FOR THE RAILHEAD IN AN HOUR. YOU'RE GOING BACK EAST WITH ME TO BE TRIED AND JUDGED BY A COURT OF YOUR PEERS.
DON'T TRY TO RUN. DON'T MAKE ME COME LOOKING FOR YOU AGAIN. I'VE ALREADY DONE MY DUE DILIGENCE TO BRING YOU IN ALIVE.
ANY MORE MISCHIEF AND I SAVE ICHABOD THE COST OF A SECOND TRAIN TICKET.

In the winter of 1883, Teddy Roosevelt killed his first buffalo, Johannes Brahms premiered his Third Symphony in F, and two German fellows, Gottlieb Daimler and Wilhelm Maybach, developed a self-propelled bicycle — the world's first motorcycle.

And an unnamed sheriff from the East forever put an end to Jack Candle and his depredations across the Wild West.

--FIND YOU *GUILTY* OF ALL CHARGES AND SENTENCE YOU TO *FIFTY YEARS* OF HARD LABOR UP AT--

NEXT: WE RETURN TO THE PRESENT DAY WITH A WHOLE NEW STORYLINE--"TURNING PAGES." IT GETS A LITTLE GIRLY IN PLACES, BUT THERE ARE ALSO SOME HALF-NAKED BROADS IN IT, SO THERE'S SOMETHING FOR EVERYONE. PLUS: WICKED JOHN IS TRANSPORTED TO MARS, WHERE HE MARRIES A GIANT GREEN HAMSTER-CREATURE.

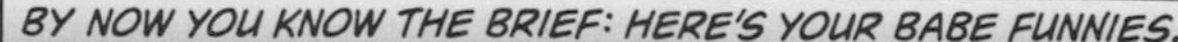
BY NOW YOU KNOW THE BRIEF: HERE'S YOUR BABE FUNNIES.

AND SO, WITH THE WIDOW KESSLER'S FARM SAFE, THE CATTLE RUSTLERS OFF TO FACE TRIAL, AND MEAN DICK ANGSTROM PUSHING UP DAISIES, IT'S TIME FOR ALOISIUS THE KID TO RIDE OFF INTO THE SUNSET.

NOT HEEDING HIS MOTHER'S OFT-GIVEN ADVICE, HOWEVER, ALOISIUS STARES DIRECTLY INTO THE SUNSET THE ENTIRE WAY.

AFTER AN HOUR OR SO, HE CAN'T SEE ANYTHING EXCEPT FOR BIG ORANGE BLOTCHES, WHICH IS HOW HE MANAGES TO MISS THE TURN TO KANSAS CITY AND RIDE DIRECTLY INTO A DEEP, TREACHEROUS RAVINE.
FILLED WITH SHARP ROCKS. AND RATTLESNAKES.

NOW BLIND, COVERED IN BRUISES AND SNAKEBITES, AND DOWN TO THE LAST SIP OF STALE WATER IN HIS CANTEEN, ALOISIUS IS FORCED TO CONSIDER THAT RIDING OFF INTO THE SUNSET MIGHT NOT HAVE BEEN THE BEST IDEA.

IF HE SOMEHOW MANAGES TO SURVIVE THE NIGHT, ALOISIUS PLEDGES, HE'S ONLY GOING TO RIDE OFF AFTER BRUNCH FROM NOW ON.

HELLO, MY NAME IS ELIZA WALL.

I'D LIKE TO TELL YOU A STORY.

YOU DON'T KNOW ME, BY THE WAY. I'M USUALLY ***QUITE*** INVISIBLE, SO THERE'S NO USE DIGGING THROUGH BACK ISSUES OR SCOURING THE INTERNET TO DISCOVER MY IDENTITY.

I LIVE HERE WITH MY THREE BROTHERS, WHO ***THEMSELVES*** ARE SO ***COMMONPLACE*** THAT YOU'D SCARCELY NOTICE THEM.

BUT WHO I AM DOESN'T MATTER. I'M NOT HERE TO TELL YOU ABOUT MYSELF.

THE STORY I'M GOING TO TELL YOU IS CALLED "TURNING PAGES," AND AS YOU MAY HAVE GUESSED, THIS TITLE IS A DOUBLE-ENTENDRE, REFERRING BOTH TO THE ACT OF ***READING*** AND TO MY YOUNG ***COUSINS,*** OFTEN REFERRED TO COLLECTIVELY AS THE PAGE SISTERS.

IT'S NOT THEIR STORY, OF COURSE. THEY'RE DOOMED TO BE SUPPORTING CHARACTERS IN SOMEONE ELSE'S DRAMA, AS WE ALL ARE FROM TIME TO TIME.

SOMEWHERE IN THE ROCKY MOUNTAINS OF COLORADO.
MOTEL
HISP'R
PINES

THIS IS ROBIN PAGE, MY YOUNG RELATION.
IF YOU'VE BEEN KEEPING UP, THEN YOU KNOW THAT ROBIN WORKS AT THE GOLDEN BOUGHS RETIREMENT COMMUNITY, A PLACE WHERE FABLES ARE BROUGHT TO FADE AWAY.

ROBIN IS IN CHARGE OF SECURITY THERE, AND--WITH ONE GLARING EXCEPTION--HAS ALWAYS DONE A COMMENDABLE JOB.
MOTEL
WH
P
YOU SEE, A FEW MONTHS AGO, ROBIN MADE WHAT MAY WELL HAVE BEEN THE WORST MISTAKE OF HER SUPERNATURALLY LONG LIFE.

AND NOW HERE SHE IS, UNABLE TO HELP HERSELF, ABOUT TO COMPOUND THE MISTAKE FURTHER.

I CAN'T BELIEVE I'M ABOUT TO DO THIS.
203

HOW DID IT COME TO THIS?
WELL. WHEN THE PAGE SISTERS WERE LITTLE GIRLS, ROBIN WAS ALWAYS THE ONE IN CHARGE.
NO! I'M THE ASSISTANT LIBRARIAN AND YOU TWO ARE THE RENEGADE FABLES!
WHY DO WE ALWAYS HAVE TO BE THE FABLES?

AS SHE BLOSSOMED INTO A YOUNG WOMAN, ROBIN WAS OFTEN THE CENTER OF ATTENTION--AND SHE LIKED IT THAT WAY.
THAT CREEP WICKED JOHN KEEPS OGLING YOU. YOU WANT ME TO HIT HIM AGAIN?
LET HIM LOOK, DEAR. LET HIM LOOK.

AND AS FAR AS HER RELATIONSHIPS WITH MEN WENT--WELL, LET'S JUST SAY SHE LIKED TO BE IN CHARGE THERE AS WELL.
WHEN CAN WE DO THIS AGAIN?
AGAIN? YOU BARELY DID IT THIS TIME.
BROOMS

YES, ROBIN ENJOYED BEING IN CHARGE--WHICH MADE HER CHOICE OF VOCATION AS MISTER REVISE'S HEAD SKULL-CRACKER A NO-BRAINER.
YOU CALL THIS AN ESCAPE ATTEMPT, MISTER D?
MAYBE NEXT TIME I'LL OPEN THE GATES AND GIVE YOU A THREE-HOUR HEAD START--JUST TO MAKE IT HALFWAY INTERESTING.
LET MY PEOPLE GO! WE SHALL OVERCOME! I HAVE A DREAM!

SO IMAGINE ROBIN'S SURPRISE WHEN SHE SUDDENLY FOUND HERSELF CAUGHT OFF GUARD.
WHAT ARE *YOU* DOING HERE?

IMAGINE HER SHOCK WHEN SHE DISCOVERED THAT FOR THE FIRST TIME IN HER LIFE SHE WAS *OUT OF CONTROL*--
MMMM.
AND *LOVING IT.*
OH, PLEASE PLEASE DON'T STOP!

SO WHAT HAPPENED-- OR SHOULD WE SAY *WHO* HAPPENED-- TO ROBIN PAGE?
HEY, BABY.

WELL, THIS DOUCHEBAG, OF COURSE. WHO ELSE?
DON'T TELL ME YOU DIDN'T SEE THAT ONE COMING.
IT IS HIS NAME ON THE COVER, AFTER ALL.
OH GOD, I LOVE YOU, JACK!
I MISSED YOU SO MUCH!
RIGHT BACK ATCHA, SWEETHEART.
203
SSNOORT

ALONSO THE CRUELTY-FREE PIRATE AND HIS GENTLE CREW HAVE JUST CAPTURED A FAT MERCHANT GALLEON LOADED WITH ENVIRONMENTALLY FRIENDLY CARGO.

ALONSO STANDS ON THE QUARTERDECK, SURVEYING HIS MEN AS THEY BREAK THE MERCHANT MARINES INTO SMALL GROUPS FOR SHORT-TERM COUNSELING.

ALONSO REASSURES THESE POOR SOULS IN HIS KINDEST VOICE THAT THEY SHOULD NOT SUFFER ANY LOW SELF-ESTEEM FOR HAVING SUCCUMBED TO HIS WILY ATTACK.

UNLIKE LESS SENSITIVE PIRATES--ALONSO DOES NOT FORCE HIS CAPTIVES TO WALK THE PLANK.
INSTEAD HE PUTS THEM IN THE GALLEON'S LIFEBOATS AND POINTS THEM TO SHORE, WHILE HIS FIRST MATE HANDS OUT SANDWICHES.

BUT ALONSO THE CRUELTY-FREE PIRATE IS NO BARBARIAN--HE MAKES SURE TO TRIM THE CRUSTS FIRST.

THE GOLDEN BOUGHS RETIREMENT COMMUNITY.

AH, THERE'S NO PLACE LIKE HOME.
GO TO HELL!
HEY, WATCH IT, YA BIG JERK!

GERTIE! HEY, BABE!
TED!
WELCOME BACK, PRISCILLA.
HOME. RIGHT.

WELCOME BACK, DOT.
HEY, T.W.
TELL MUELLER IN THE MOTOR POOL THE NEXT TIME I TAKE OUT A VAN WITH AN EMPTY GAS TANK HE'S GOING TO FIND HIMSELF SHOVELING DRAGON SHIT FOR A LIVING.

AND MAKE SURE ROBIN IS NOTIFIED ABOUT THE NEW ARRIVAL.
ROBIN IS ON VACATION, MA'AM. IN THE MUNDY.

...AND SHE WAS REALLY TRYING TO PUT ON A ONE-WOMAN SHOW ABOUT THE LIFE OF JUDY GARLAND?
YEP, AND THE BEST PART IS, SHE CAN'T EVEN SING.

DON'T SUPPOSE YOU'VE HEARD FROM HILLARY?
HEAD LIBRARIAN
NOT A PEEP IN THREE MONTHS. AND DON'T SAY THAT NAME WITHIN A HUNDRED YARDS OF THIS OFFICE IF YOU LIKE YOUR JOB.
OKAY, LET'S SEE WHAT I'M GOING TO GET MY ASS RIPPED FOR TODAY.

PRISCILLA.
THE SWEET SMELL OF SUCCESS!
NOT BAD, EH?

MM.
HI, PRISCILLA.
HI, KEVIN.

WELL?
YOU SPENT TWO WEEKS ON THE ROAD AND YOU MANAGED TO APPREHEND ONLY A SINGLE FABLE, ONE WHO MIGHT AS WELL HAVE BEEN WEARING A SIGN THAT SAID, "PLEASE CATCH ME."

WITH ALL DUE RESPECT, SIR--WE'VE MADE STRIDES! I'VE RETRIEVED A NUMBER OF SIGNIFICANT FABLES IN THE PAST YEAR.

A SMALL NUMBER, YES. WHILE JACK OF THE TALES WALKS FREE. WHILE OLD SAM WALKS FREE. WHILE THE PATHETIC FALLACY WALKS FREE.

I THOUGHT I COULD COUNT ON YOU, PRISCILLA. YOU USED TO BE THE ONE I COULD TRUST. YOU USED TO BE THE RELIABLE ONE.
BUT EVER SINCE JACK OF THE TALES CAME INTO OUR LIVES, YOU'VE BEEN DISTRACTED AND UNRELIABLE.

YOU'VE PROVEN TO BE A GRAVE DISAPPOINTMENT, PRISCILLA.
YOU'RE SUSPENDED UNTIL FURTHER NOTICE.

GERTRUDE CAN RUN THINGS WHILE YOU FIGURE OUT HOW TO BECOME USEFUL AGAIN.

NOW IF YOU'LL EXCUSE ME, IT APPEARS I'VE GOT AN APPOINTMENT WITH THE MEMORY HOLE.
KEVIN, WE'LL CONTINUE OUR CONVERSATION AT ANOTHER TIME.
SURE THING, SON.

IT'S NOT YOUR FAULT, YOU KNOW.
IT ISN'T YOU HE'S MAD AT.
I KNOW.
I UNDER-STAND HE'S PISSED OFF AT HILLARY FOR DISAPPEARING WITHOUT A BY-YOUR-LEAVE, BUT I'M STILL HERE. I STUCK AROUND.
AND THIS IS THE THANKS I GET.

WELL, IF YOU NEED SOME-ONE TO TALK TO, I'M HERE FOR YOU. NO ONE KNOWS BETTER THAN I DO HOW DIFFICULT REVISE CAN BE.

I'M HIS FATHER AFTER ALL.

THE IDAHO WOODS.
ALL IS WELL WITH THE TROOPS, OMAR?
YES, BOOKBURNER, SIR. YONDER VALLEY MEETS OUR HUMBLE REQUIREMENTS FOR A BIVOUAC.
AT THIS RATE, FOUR DAYS WILL FIND US AT THE GOLDEN BOUGHS.
FINE, OMAR. WELL DONE.
IT'S NOW OR NEVER, MISTER D.
YOU READY?
I WAS LAID READY, HONEY-CAKES.
SHUT YER YAPS, LANDLUBBERS.

ONE DIVERSION COMING UP!
AHOY, MISSY! Y'EVER MADE OUT WITH A TOOTHLESS BUCCANEER?

NOT EVEN IN MY WORST NIGHTMARES, CAP'N SCURVEY.

HEY, EVERYBODY! LOOK AT ME! LOOK AT ME!

NOW NOW, MISTER D. I BELIEVE WE HAD A TALK ABOUT THESE OUTBURSTS OF YOURS, DIDN'T WE?

OH, I'LL SHOW YOU AN OUTBURST, BUDDY!
YOU'RE ABOUT TO SEE WHAT AN OLD CANNON FROM COLCHESTER--

UH-OH.
KA-BLOOIE!!
WELL, SHIVER ME TIMBERS.

OH, NOW WHERE WAS I?
YOU'LL HAVE TO PARDON ME--I'M NOT MUCH OF A NARRATOR. LIKE I SAID, I'M USUALLY SOMEONE WHO TRIES TO GO UNNOTICED AS MUCH AS POSSIBLE.

GASSUP
GASSUP
AND AFTER ALL, WE'RE NOT HERE TO TALK ABOUT ME. WE'RE HERE TO TALK ABOUT ROBIN.

I NEED TO MAKE A COLLECT CALL, PLEASE!

HEH. GUESS I MISFIRED.

OMAR, I WANT EVERY LAST PIECE OF THIS DAMNED EGG PICKED UP IN TWENTY MINUTES, DO YOU HEAR ME?
I'LL PUT THE CROWS AND THE MICE ON IT, SIR.

UM, ER, EXCUSE ME, YER HONOR, BUT...
CAP'N SCURVEY!

WHERE IS HILLARY PAGE?!
AND JACK, OF COURSE. IF WE MUST.

JACK HORNER, AS YOU KNOW, IS SOMETHING OF A CAD.
DINER
DINER
AND THEN WITH NO PROVOCATION WHATSOEVER, HILLARY AND THE EGG TRIED TO ROB ME BLIND.
AND SHE TRIED TO KILL ME, TOO! FOR NO REASON!

A LIAR, TOO. BUT--AS IS OFTEN THE WAY WITH MEN LIKE HIM--INEXPLICABLY GOOD WITH WOMEN.
OH, THAT LITTLE BRAT!
HILLARY ALWAYS WAS A PROBLEM CHILD.

AND SO WHAT NOW, BABY? IS IT TIME TO RUN OFF TO THE BAHAMAS AND SPEND ALL THAT DIRTY MONEY?
JUST SOMETHING ABOUT BAD BOYS, I SUPPOSE.

WHA-- SPEND? OH, HELL NO, WOMAN!

OH, GREAT SPIRIT. HERE WE GO AGAIN.
LISTEN, SWEETHEART. EVERY SINGLE TIME I'VE COME INTO MONEY, SOMETHING'S ALWAYS GONE WRONG.
AND I'VE FINALLY FIGURED OUT WHAT IT IS.

SEE, EVERY TIME I GET MONEY, I START SPENDING IT.
LIKE THAT PONZI GUY, BACK IN BOSTON. DID I WALK AWAY WITH MY DIVIDENDS? NO, LIKE A FOOL I REINVESTED-- AND LOOK HOW THAT TURNED OUT!

OR THAT TIME I WON A HUNDRED GRAND FROM BLUEBEARD AT POKER. DID I KEEP THE MONEY? NO! I BLEW IT ALL ON AN INTERNET CHEESE STARTUP!
eCHEESE! WHAT WAS I THINKING?

SO NOW THAT I'VE FINALLY STRUCK IT RICH, I'M GOING TO DO THE ONLY SENSIBLE THING:
NEVER SPEND A PENNY OF IT. EVER.

BUT, SWEETIE. WHAT'S THE POINT OF HAVING IT IF WE NEVER SPEND ANY OF IT?

HAVEN'T YOU HEARD A WORD I JUST SAID?
breet breet
OH, HANG ON.

OH, IT'S YOU.
YOU'VE GOT A LOT OF NERVE CALLING ME, LITTLE SIS, AFTER EVERYTHING YOU'VE--

YOU WHAT?
HOLY SHIT!!

WHAT WAS THAT ALL ABOUT?
THAT WAS HILLARY. SHE--IT'S BOOKBURNER. IT'S THE GODDAMNED BOOK-BURNER!
AND HE'S HERE. IN THE MUNDY!
HE'S COMING FOR THE GOLDEN BOUGHS!

THAT GUY? SO WHAT?
LONG AS HE'S NOT COMING FOR US, ROBIN, BABY, WHAT DO I CARE?
JACK, YOU DON'T GET IT.

IF HE MANAGES TO TAKE THE GOLDEN BOUGHS, YOU'RE DEAD.
EVERY FABLE EVERYWHERE IS DEAD!

THE GOLDEN BOUGHS.
The Fox & Grapes
IT'S THAT SON OF A BITCH, JACK HORNER!
EVER SINCE HE CAME INTO MY LIFE, EVERYTHING'S GONE TO SHIT!
TELL ME ABOUT IT. NOT ONLY DID HE MANIPULATE AND OBJECTIFY ME, BUT I THINK HE ALSO GAVE ME CRABS.
IF I EVER GET MY HANDS ON THAT BASTARD, I'LL SHAVE HIS HEAD AND STRANGLE HIM WITH HIS OWN HAIR.
PRIS, IF I EVER GET MY HANDS ON HIM, I'D CASTRATE HIM WITH A PAIR OF RUSTY GARDEN SHEARS AND DO THE WORLD A FAVOR.
YOU SAID IT, GOLDIE.
I'D SWALLOW HIS BRAINS FOR HATRED'S SAKE.
AND FROM HIS EMPTY SKULL A GOBLET MAKE.
LUCKY, REMEMBER WHEN WE TALKED ABOUT "TAKING IT TOO FAR"?
breet breet
AW, DAMMIT! THIS IS MY NIGHT OFF!

BUT THOU DID SPEAK TO THY DESIRE TO UNMAN!
THERE ARE DEGREES, LUCKY.
HELLO?

THE BOOKBURNER. HE'S IN THE MUNDY!
IS HE A FABLE? I'VE NEVER HEARD OF HIM.
NOT EXACTLY.

NO FABLE HE--BUT LITERAL. I FLED AMERICANA AND BARELY 'SCAPED HIS FLAME--

TREMBLE DO I AT THE HEARING OF THE NAME.

CLAK

WELL, THIS IS AN AWKWARD MOMENT, ISN'T IT?

GO TO HELL!

UNH!

I'M AFRAID YOU'RE COMING BACK WITH ME, YOUNG LADY.
LIKE IT OR NOT.

YES, A GIRL IN LOVE WILL DO MANY THINGS SHE OUGHTN'T.
JACK, YOU DON'T UNDERSTAND. BOOKBURNER IS A MONSTER! REVISE USED TO TELL US STORIES ABOUT BOOKBURNER TO SCARE US AS KIDS.
NO, BABE-- YOU DON'T UNDERSTAND. THERE'S STILL SOME SANDWICH ON THAT PLATE!

SHE'LL PUT UP WITH ALL SORTS OF NONSENSE FROM HER BELOVED.
BY THE WAY, ROBIN, CAN YOU GET THIS ONE? I LEFT MY WALLET BACK AT THE MOTEL.

SHE'LL EVEN RUN AWAY FROM HOME TO BE WITH HIM.
LISTEN!
IF BOOKBURNER GETS TO THE GOLDEN BOUGHS, HE WON'T JUST KILL REVISE AND ALL OF THE FABLES LIVING THERE.

BUT ROBIN PAGE HAS BEEN IN SECURITY A LOT LONGER THAN SHE'S BEEN IN LOVE.
IF HE GETS HOLD OF REVISE'S LIBRARY, HE'LL KILL ALL OF YOU. EVERY FABLE EVERYWHERE.
THAT'S WHAT HE WANTS. THAT'S ALL HE WANTS.

THIS COULD WORK OUT.

AND A *PAGE SISTER* FIRST.

--I HAVE TO GO ACHIEVE FAME AND GLORY AS THEIR ANOINTED *HERO!*

NEXT: *I WROTE A BUNCH OF BRILLIANT CAPTIONS FOR THIS ISSUE, AND NOW LOOKING BACK OVER IT, I SEE THEY'VE ALL BEEN REPLACED BY SOME* ***BROAD--*** *WITH EMOTIONS AND MEANINGFUL FLASHBACKS AND ALL THAT CRAP. YOU BETTER BELIEVE THAT THERE ARE GOING TO BE SOME CHANGES AROUND HERE NEXT MONTH.* ***MANLY*** *CHANGES! WITH LASER BATTLES, MONSTER TRUCKS, AND GIRLS IN BIKINIS WRESTLING WITH CHEETAHS. STICK WITH IT, BOYS!*

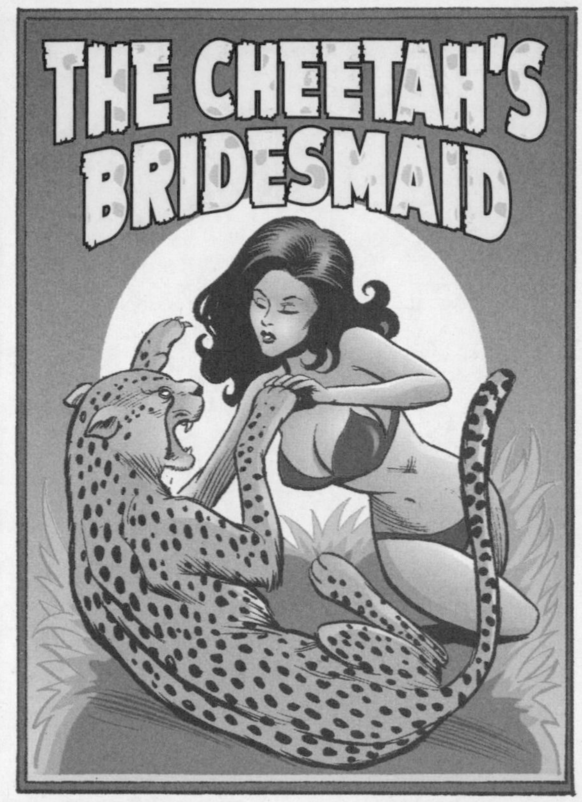

UNFORTUNATELY FOR THOSE OF YOU WHO CONTINUED READING ***BASED*** ON THOSE PROMISES, THE CURRENT CHAPTER CONTAINS ***NO SUCH*** ELEMENTS.

LASER
NEW Y

TURNING PAGES: CHAPTER TWO

THIS CHAPTER PROMINENTLY FEATURES MY YOUNG NIECE ***PRISCILLA PAGE.***

AND WHILE PRIS ***IS*** A GIRL, AND ***HAS*** BEEN KNOWN TO WEAR A BIKINI ON ***OCCASION,*** I DON'T BELIEVE SHE'S ***EVER*** WRESTLED A CHEETAH.

NOT THAT SHE WOULDN'T TRY.

PRISCILLA

PRISCILLA AND ROBIN WERE BORN ON THE SAME DAY, ONLY MINUTES APART. GROWING UP, THEY WERE BOTH HEADSTRONG, CLEVER, AND RESOURCEFUL.
IT WAS HER IDEA!

UNFORTUNATELY FOR PRIS, THAT'S WHERE THE SIMILARITIES ENDED.
WHY, PRISCILLA! I'M MOST DISAPPOINTED!
HELLO...?
ME?

WHERE ROBIN WAS CONFIDENT AND POPULAR, PRIS NEVER QUITE FIT IN, AND FOR MOST OF HER YOUTH, THAT WAS FINE BY HER.
WHEN I GROW UP, I'M GOING TO BE THE HEAD OF SECURITY, AND I'M GOING TO HAVE A DOZEN TIGERS TO REND THE FABLES LIMB FROM LIMB! WHAT ABOUT YOU?
I WANT TO BE A MARINE BIOLOGIST AND STUDY NARWHALS. I MIGHT MARRY A NARWHAL.

ALL HER LIFE, SHE HAD BEEN TOLD THAT IF SHE WOULD JUST "BE HERSELF" THAT SHE'D DO JUST FINE IN LIFE.
BUT AS THE YEARS WENT BY, PRISCILLA BEGAN TO SUSPECT THAT THIS ADVICE WAS BULLSHIT.
HEY, RONNIE! YOU'RE SUPPOSED TO BE MY DATE, REMEMBER?

THE PROBLEM WAS THAT NOBODY SEEMED TO LIKE PRISCILLA WHEN SHE WAS "BEING HERSELF."
SO, UH, WHAT DO YOU THINK, JOE?
Staff Break Room
GEE, UM, I THINK I ALREADY HAVE A DATE FOR THE MIXER.

AND OVER TIME, PRIS BEGAN TO AGREE WITH THEM.
DUDE, NOT EVEN A NARWHAL WOULD GO WITH HER!
STUPID, STUPID, STUPID!

SO SHE TOOK WHAT--TO HER--WAS THE ONLY REASONABLE COURSE OF ACTION.
SEE? VERY SUBTLE LAYERS.

SHE BECAME SOMEONE ELSE.
HEY, BOYS!

AND IT WORKED LIKE A CHARM.
DAMN, PRIS, YOU GOT HOT. AND YOU USED TO BE SUCH A DORK!
THANKS, JOE.

EVERYONE LOVED THE NEW PRISCILLA, AND SHE DID EVERYTHING SHE COULD TO KEEP IT THAT WAY.
AND IF SOMEONE DIDN'T LOVE HER?

WELL, SHE HAD STRATEGIES IN PLACE TO REMEDY SUCH MATTERS.
PREPARE YOURSELF FOR TOTAL SATISFACTION, LOVERBOY.

YES, PRISCILLA FIGURED OUT HOW TO BE THE GIRL THAT EVERYONE LOVED.
YOU'RE LOOKING ESPECIALLY LOVELY, PRIS.
SHUT UP AND GET TO WORK!

WELL... ALMOST EVERYONE.
ESPECIALLY LOVELY, MY ASS. I LOOK LIKE A COW WITH A PERM.

HEAD LIBRARI
OKAY-- HERE WE GO.
PLAY IT COOL, SISTER.

I WANT ALL PATROLS AND GUARD DETAILS **DOUBLED!** HAVE AT LEAST ONE PLATOON OF BAGMEN DECANTED AND READY FOR **USE** AT ALL TIMES!
GET WITH ROBIN THE **INSTANT** SHE RETURNS!
N
IDAHO
SO...WHERE DO YOU WANT ME?
EH?
EXCUSE ME? THE LAST TIME WE **SPOKE** I BELIEVE I SUSPENDED YOU FROM YOUR DUTIES UNTIL FURTHER NOTICE.
I JUST FIGURED, WHAT WITH THE BOOK-BURNER COMING AND EVERYTHING, THERE MUST BE **SOMETHING** I CAN DO TO HELP.
YOU FIGURED **INCORRECTLY,** PRISCILLA, AS PER USUAL, OF LATE.

NOW, HANG ON! THAT'S JUST NOT FAIR!
I DON'T KNOW IF YOU'RE JUST PISSED BECAUSE HILLARY--
DON'T YOU DARE MENTION HER!

THEN LET ME HELP SORT THINGS OUT! I CAN TALK TO THEM.

YOU'VE DONE ENOUGH, PRISCILLA. GO HOME AND STAY THERE.

AND TRY NOT TO RUIN ANY-THING ELSE ON YOUR WAY.

UH, SIR. HAS ROBIN--
NO! ROBIN HAS NOT ARRIVED YET!

HOW DOES THE GIRL EVERYONE LOVES DEAL WITH REJECTION ON SUCH A MASSIVE SCALE? I'D TELL YOU, BUT YOU CAN SEE FOR YOURSELF IN SEVEN PAGES.
HI, PRIS.
SNIF!

HMM.
IT INVOLVES PLATES.

A FEW MILES NORTH OF OGDEN, UTAH.
GAS - FIL'R'UP - GAS
FIL'R'UP
I JUST DON'T SEE IT, DUDE. THERE'S **NO WAY** YOU'RE GOING TO PULL THIS OFF.

YOU WILLING TO **BET** ON THAT, CHIEF SITTING BULL?
I WOULD, BUT YOU'VE GOT MY SHARE OF THE **GOLD** LOCKED IN THAT MAGIC BRIEFCASE OF YOURS. AND THAT THING IS **IMPOSSIBLE** TO BREAK INTO!
UH, OR AT LEAST I WOULD **ASSUME** IT IS.

YOU'RE DAMN **RIGHT** I'VE GOT YOUR MONEY LOCKED UP, AND IT'LL STAY THAT WAY UNTIL YOU CAN SHOW ME THAT YOU'RE ABLE TO MANAGE YOUR FINANCES **RESPONSIBLY.**
WHICH **CLEARLY** ISN'T THE CASE IF YOU'RE WILLING TO BET AGAINST **ME.**
FWOOSH!

MEN
BET AGAINST HIM ON WHAT?

MEN
CASANOVA HERE THINKS HE CAN GET ALL THREE PAGE SISTERS AT THE SAME TIME.
GET THEM FOR WHAT?

GET THEM IN THE SAME ROOM SO I CAN APOLOGIZE TO THEM FOR ALL MY WICKED WAYS.
YAY!

YOU CAN'T TALK ABOUT SEX IN FRONT OF GARY.
IT MAKES HIM HYPER-VENTILATE.
LOOK, ROBIN!

I FOUND TURKEY JERKY!
OKAY, GREAT. CAN WE PLEASE GET GOING NOW?

YOU DO NOT WANT TO BE IN THE CAR WITH ME IF I'VE BEEN EATING BEEF JERKY.

SOMEWHERE OUTSIDE OF POCATELLO, IDAHO.
OKAY, LET'S TALK TACTICS, SWEETIE.
I KNOW YOU'VE FOUGHT IN SEVERAL WARS--

--AND GARY TELLS ME THAT YOU WERE THE KEY STRATEGIST IN DEFENDING FABLETOWN AGAINST THE ADVERSARY'S WOODEN SOLDIERS, SO I THINK WE SHOULD--

MMMM, JERKY...
snort!
RELAX, HONEY PUPS.

I'VE GONE TOE-TO-TOE WITH THIS LOSER ONCE BEFORE, AND HE'S A PUSHOVER.
I DON'T SEE WHAT YOU FOLKS ARE GETTING SO UP IN ARMS ABOUT, TO BE HONEST.

JACK, I'M NOT SURE YOU'RE GETTING--
WE'LL TRUSS UP BOOKBURNER LICKETY-SPLIT, AND THEN YOU AND ME AND MAYBE YOUR SISTERS ALL HIT THE HOT TUB TOGETHER.

SO, UH, JUST HOW CLOSE ARE YOU AND YOUR SISTERS, ANYWAY?

CRASH GANESVOORT COULD TELL YOU STORIES ABOUT HIS YEARS AS A SPECIAL OPS MIME IN THE FRENCH FOREIGN LEGION.
STORIES THAT WOULD TURN THE BLOOD IN YOUR VEINS TO ICEWATER.
SPUD

LIKE THE MISSION IN TUNISIA, WHEN HE WITNESSED HIS ENTIRE PLATOON CUT DOWN BY ENEMY FIRE WHILE HE WATCHED HELPLESSLY FROM INSIDE AN INVISIBLE CAGE--
--PUSHING AGAINST THE WALLS IN A VAIN ATTEMPT TO ESCAPE.
SPUD

CRASH STILL HAS NIGHTMARES ABOUT THAT FATEFUL DAY IN ALGERIA.
HE REMEMBERS THE WINDS, SO STRONG THAT HE WALKED AGAINST THEM WITHOUT MOVING FOR WHAT SEEMED LIKE HOURS, WHILE THE EXPLOSIONS RANG OUT AROUND HIM.
SPUD

IN MADAGASCAR, THEY TORTURED CRASH FOR WEEKS, USING THE MOST CRUEL METHODS KNOWN TO MANKIND, BUT NO MATTER WHAT THEY DID, CRASH DIDN'T SAY A WORD.
SPUD

SERIOUSLY THOUGH, IF THOSE MUMMENSCHANZ POSEURS DON'T STEP OFF, CRASH IS GOING TO HAVE TO CUT THEM.
SPUD

NOT TOO FAR FROM THE GOLDEN BOUGHS.
WE'RE GETTING CLOSE, HILLARY. I CAN SMELL IT.
FOR THE LAST TIME, I'M NOT GOING TO HELP YOU.
YOU THINK I'M JUST GOING TO WALK YOU RIGHT UP TO THE FRONT GATE? THE VILLAGE IS SURROUNDED BY EXTREMELY POWERFUL MAGIC DESIGNED SPECIFICALLY TO KEEP PEOPLE LIKE YOU OUT.
OH, YOU'LL HELP ME.
UNH!
TELL ME ABOUT THE DEFENSES, HILLARY. ALL OF THEM.
KILLING PEOPLE ISN'T JUST MY JOB, IT'S WHAT I ENJOY. I WON'T SHRINK FROM HURTING YOU IN THE MOST AWFUL WAYS.
UNFF!

WHAT'S REVISE GOT? DOUBLING ROOKS?
I DON'T SUPPOSE HE EVER TOLD YOU THAT I INVENTED THOSE THINGS?

WHAT ABOUT THOSE BAGMEN OF HIS? DID HE EVER GET THAT LOATHSOME LITTLE EXPERIMENT OFF THE GROUND?

SCREW YOU.

OH, FOR PETE'S SAKE! WHERE'S THE YOUNG SPITFIRE WHO KARATE-CHOPPED HER WAY OUT OF MY LIBRARY?
SIR, ONE OF OUR SPOTTERS GLIMPSED A CAR COMING DOWN THE MAIN HIGHWAY.
IT'S THEM.

WELL, WELL, WELL. HOW DO YOU LIKE THOSE APPLES?

SMASH!
WHOA, *SOMEONE'S* IN THE MIDDLE OF A CATHARSIS!
CAN YOU SAY "REPRESSED ANGER"?

CAN YOU SAY "*DADDY ISSUES*"?
YAHH!
SMASH!

LET'S FACE IT. MY NIECE--WHATEVER HER *FAVORABLE* QUALITIES--IS A CERTIFIABLE TYPE-A HEADCASE.
KNOCK KNOCK

HI, PRIS. CAN I COME IN FOR A MINUTE?
WHY NOT? IT'S NOT LIKE EITHER ONE OF US HAS ANYTHING *BETTER* TO DO.
BOOKBURNER'S COMING! WE'RE *DOOMED!*

AND WE LITERALS AREN'T EXACTLY KNOWN FOR BEING PARTICULARLY SANE, ESPECIALLY YOURS TRULY.
SO, COMING FROM ME, THAT'S SAYING SOMETHING.
KEVIN, WHAT ARE YOU DOING HERE?

SHOULD I EVEN ASK WHAT THIS IS ALL ABOUT?

STRIDENT ANTI-CONSUMERISM.
WHAT CAN I DO FOR YOU?

LISTEN, I NEED YOUR HELP.
IT'S IMPOR-TANT.

WHAT IS IT?
CAN WE TALK SOMEPLACE ELSE? I JUST WANT TO BE SURE...

NOW, IF YOU'VE BEEN PAYING ATTENTION, YOU KNOW THAT GARY--THE PATHETIC FALLACY, GRANDDADDY OF ALL US LITERALS--DOESN'T REMEMBER MUCH.
WAS THIS REALLY NECESSARY?
WAIT-- YOU'RE NOT ABOUT TO PROPOSE OR ANYTHING, ARE YOU?
LISTEN, THIS COULD GET REALLY UGLY, THIS BUSINESS BETWEEN BOOKBURNER AND REVISE.

YEAH, THAT IS THE GENERAL IMPRESSION I'M GETTING.
NO, I MEAN IT COULD GET REALLY, REALLY UGLY.
LOTS OF PEOPLE COULD GET KILLED--FABLES, LITERALS, EVEN MUNDIES IF IT GETS TOO MUCH OUT OF CONTROL.
BUT KEVIN'S BEEN DOWN THE MEMORY HOLE, TOO. WHAT DOES HE REMEMBER?

REVISE AND BOOKBURNER REALLY DESPISE EACH OTHER. THEY HAVE... HISTORY.
THEY'RE BOTH EXTREMELY POWERFUL, AND NEITHER OF THEM IS GOING TO BACK DOWN IF THEY COME TO LOGGERHEADS.

WHY ARE YOU TELLING ME THIS?
BECAUSE YOU CAN HELP ME GET OUT OF HERE. THERE'S SOMETHING I NEED.
SOMETHING THAT CAN HELP US.

WHAT? YOU EXPECT ME TO JUST--
PRIS, REVISE IS LOSING IT. SURELY YOU'VE SEEN THAT.
AND WHAT DOES HE REALLY WANT OUT OF LIFE?

WELL, I'M CERTAINLY NOT GOING TO TELL YOU. YOU'LL JUST HAVE TO KEEP ON READING TO FIND OUT.
REVISE REALLY CARES FOR HILLARY. HIS ONLY DAUGHTER DISAPPEARS MONTHS AGO, AND NOW SUDDENLY SHE SHOWS UP IN BOOKBURNER'S HANDS? THAT'S A LOT FOR A FATHER TO TAKE.

HILLARY? BUT REVISE ISN'T HILLARY'S FATHER.
OUR FATHER DIED BEFORE WE WERE BORN!

SO THAT'S WHAT HE TOLD YOU, HUH?

NO, PRISCILLA, REVISE IS DEFINITELY HILLARY'S FATHER.
NOT YOURS, THOUGH. YOU AND ROBIN HAVE A DIFFERENT FATHER.

OH, RIGHT. SO, WHO'S MY FATHER, THEN? BOOKBURNER?

UM, ACTUALLY?

YEAH.

AND NOW, THE FINAL SCENE OF THIS CHAPTER. AND YOU MAY NOTE THAT THERE'S NOT A MONSTER TRUCK OR BIKINI-CLAD CHEETAH-WRESTLER IN SIGHT.
HERE WE GO--TURN RIGHT HERE.
TOLD YOU.

LISTEN, JACK. WHEN WE GET BACK TO THE GOLDEN BOUGHS, JUST LET ME HANDLE IT.
I'LL WORK OUT EVERYTHING WITH REVISE. IT'LL BE AWKWARD, BUT I JUST KNOW THAT IT'LL ALL WORK OUT.
NO PROBLEM, SUGAR. I ESCAPED ONCE--I CAN DO IT AGAIN IF I HAVE TO.

OF COURSE, WHEN WE GET MARRIED, YOU MAY WANT TO COME LIVE WITH ME AT THE GOLDEN BOUGHS!

SURE, PEOPLE WILL SCOFF. "A FABLE AND A LITERAL--THAT'S PREPOSTEROUS!" THEY'LL SAY.
BUT OUR LOVE WILL TRIUMPH OVER ALL.

DON'T YOU THINK?
UH-- HEY, DID YOU SEE THAT?

DID YOU FIGURE OUT WHO THE SHADOWY FIGURE IS YET? THIS SHOULD GIVE IT AWAY.

HEH. DO YA OVER EASY.

WHAT THE HELL?!

SKRUNK!

EEEEEEP!
THUD!
OOF!
CRASH!

WHO *WAS* THAT?
I DON'T KNOW, BUT HE'S IN BIG, *BIG* TROUBLE.

OKAY, GET READY FOR IT. YOU'RE ALMOST AT THE LAST PAGE, SO YOU KNOW THERE'S GOING TO BE A *BIG REVEAL*.
I SICKED UP MY TURKEY JERKY!
THAT'S WHAT WE'VE BEEN TAUGHT.

A FEELING OF *RISING* DREAD...
UH, JACK?
I DON'T LIKE THIS AT ALL.
THE SHOCK OF DAWNING REALIZATION (UNLESS YOU WERE CLEVER AND FIGURED IT OUT TWO PAGES AGO).
HEY, GUYS! LOOK AT *ME*!
THEY PUT ME BACK *TOGETHER* AGAIN!
HERE IT COMES...

BIG FINISH!
BUT THEY TURNED ME INTO A DEVILED EGG THIS TIME.
AND I LIKE IT!!
I DON'T KNOW WHO THIS NEW NARRATOR BROAD IS, BUT SHE'S TURNING MY BOOK INTO SOME KIND OF WEIRD POST-MODERN CHICK-LIT, AND THAT'S NOT SOMETHING I CAN LET PASS. FORTUNATELY, THE NEXT ISSUE IS A "DONE-IN-ONE" STORY ABOUT ME FIGHTING EVIL ALIENS, TRYING TO REACH THEIR SLIME-COVERED HOMEWORLD TO FIND A CURE FOR GARY BEFORE THE UFO QUEEN'S LARVAE HATCH IN HIS EYEBALLS AND TURN HIM INTO SOME KIND OF STUMBLING, EYELESS SPACE-ZOMBIE. I'D LIKE TO SEE HER TRY TO MOCK THAT!

'BYE, DEX! SEE YOU IN A BIT!
Ã BIENTÔT, MA CHERE!
OH, HI THERE. SORRY FOR THE INTERRUPTION, BUT THERE'S A LOT GOING ON.
THIS IS MY LAST ISSUE AND I WANT TO MAKE SURE I GET EVERY-THING IN.
JACK! NO! YOU CAN'T BE DEAD!
SEE, I'M NOT JUST THE NARRATOR--I ALSO HAVE A PART TO PLAY IN THE STORY, HOWEVER SMALL.
I HAVE TO KEEP THIS FROM HAPPENING, EVEN THOUGH I'M NOT REALLY INCLINED TO DO SO.
JACK! NO! YOU CAN'T BE DEAD!
BUT ENOUGH ABOUT HIM. I'M HERE TODAY TO TALK TO YOU ABOUT SOME-ONE I MUCH PREFER.
HER NAME IS HILLARY PAGE.

THE MAIN THING YOU NEED TO KNOW ABOUT HILLARY IS THAT ALL HER LIFE SHE'S HAD A SECRET FANTASY.
IT'S A DREAM THAT'S TABOO AMONG THE LITERALS.
HILLARY, YOU SEE, HAS ALWAYS DREAMED...
...OF BEING A FABLE.
OH, FAIR PRINCE--LET US BE MARRIED UPON THE 'MORROW!
TURNING PAGES
Chapter Three: HILLARY

IT ALL STARTED WITH BOOKS.
HILLARY DIDN'T JUST LIKE BOOKS--SHE ADORED THEM. HISTORY, GEOGRAPHY, POETRY, SCIENCE FICTION, YOU NAME IT.
RESTRICT MATERIA EYES ONL
TALES OF THE GROTESQUE
EDGAR
THE MABINOGION
HOMER THE ILIA
WITH HER NOSE IN A BOOK, HILLARY COULD SHUT OUT THE WORLD AROUND HER ALTOGETHER.

HILL, ARE YOU A STUPID NINNY?
ARE YOU A SMELLY BRAT?
UH-HUH.
JAMES JOYCE
ulysses

IF EVER ANYONE WAS BORN TO BE A LIBRARIAN, IT WAS HILLARY.
HILLARY HAD BEEN BROUGHT UP TO BELIEVE THAT THE GOLDEN BOUGHS WAS A PLACE WHERE FABLES WERE BROUGHT FOR THEIR OWN GOOD--

--AND OH, HOW SHE WANTED TO FIND EVERY LAST ONE OF THEM!
GRIMM'S GEOGRAPHY
SEARCH OF... AVALON
MYTHIK AMERIKA
Fabletown! but where?
B.B.W.?
S.W.?
LRRH?

SHE STALKED THEM TIRELESSLY THROUGH BOOKS AND MAGAZINES AND NEWSPAPERS. IF SHE COULDN'T BE A FABLE, AT LEAST SHE COULD SURROUND HERSELF WITH THEM.
PLEASE?
SIGH "CURIOUSER AND CURIOUSER."
CAN I GO NOW?

SHE EVEN BELIEVED (ERRONEOUSLY) THAT SHE MIGHT SOMEDAY FALL IN LOVE WITH ONE.

BUT WE'RE GETTING AHEAD OF OURSELVES.
BECAUSE IT WAS THE DAY SHE DISCOVERED MISTER BURNER'S LETTERS TO HER MOTHER--THE ORIGINAL MISS PAGE--THAT HILLARY'S HIDDEN DREAMS BEGAN TO WRECK HER LIFE.
WORD. BABE

REVISE CALLED BURNER A MONSTER, AND CLAIMED THAT HE LIVED TO DESTROY ALL OF FABLEKIND. BUT IN HIS LETTERS, A VERY DIFFERENT MAN PRESENTED HIMSELF.
IN HIS LETTERS, HE WAS A LIBRARIAN. HE CARED ABOUT BOOKS AND FABLES. AND AS HE WAS CLEARLY VERY MUCH IN LOVE WITH THE ORIGINAL MISS PAGE, IT ONLY STOOD TO REASON.
I'M YOUR DAUGHTER!

GUESS NOT.
STILL THINK I'M YOUR DADDY NOW, SWEETIE?
AND THAT PRETTY MUCH BRINGS US UP-TO-DATE ON POOR HILLARY.
SO LET'S SEE WHAT'S GOING ON WITH OUR TITULAR CHARACTER.
BY THE WAY-- HAVE YOU EVER NOTICED THAT IF YOU RUN THE TITLE TOGETHER, IT BECOMES "JACK-OFFABLES"?
I KNOW--ICK, RIGHT?

WELL, THAT CAN'T BE GOOD.
YEEEA-AARRRG-GGGH!

I'M GONNA POP HIM LIKE A ZIT!
ULK-K! DO SOME-THING!
MISTER D! WHAT HAPPENED TO YOU?
HANG ON, JACK!

I'LL SCRAMBLE YOU, PATHETIC FUCKWAD!
G-GAK-GARY!

EEEEEEP!

NAW, I KNOW! I'LL SAY SOMETHING LIKE, "JACK, YOU'RE A LOUSY FRIEND!"
AND THEN YOU GO, "AW, YOU DON'T HAVE TO BITE MY HEAD OFF."
AND THEN I BITE YOUR HEAD OFF.

GET IT? THE WHOLE FIGURATIVE-LITERAL THING?

THAT'S ENOUGH, CHICKENSPAWN!

BLAM! BLAM! BLAM!

AUGGGH! YOU KILLED ME!

JUST KIDDING!
I'M A KIDDER! I KID! IT'S WHAT I DO!

AND WHILE ALL THAT IS GOING ON, LET'S SEE WHAT'S HAPPENING BACK AT THE GOLDEN BOUGHS.
IT'S STARTING, HATTER! MAKE HASTE! MAKE HASTE!
16
I MADE SOME HASTE EARLIER IN THE EVENING, SIR HARE, JUST TO BE SAFE. AND I PUT IT IN MY HAT FOR SAFEKEEPING.
BUT I GOT PECKISH AFTER TEA AND BAKED IT UP INTO A PUDDING.
AH, I DO SO ADORE A GOOD HASTY PUDDING!
HUSH IT!
LET'S BEGIN! I BELIEVE YOU'VE ALL MET MY PARTNER, LADY LUCK?
DG
WELL, THIS DEFINITELY CAN'T BE GOOD.
BY NOW YOU'VE ALL HEARD THAT THE OPPRESSOR REVISE STANDS AT THE EVE OF HIS OWN UNDOING.
HIS NEMESIS--A MAN CALLED BOOKBURNER--IS EVEN NOW MARCHING ON THE GATES OF OUR GULAG! AND THIS IS THE OPPOR-TUNITY WE'VE BEEN WAITING FOR!
DORMOUSE! WAKE UP! I BELIEVE SHE'S TALKING ABOUT A REVOLU-TION!
I'M MUCH TOO SLEEPY TO REVOLVE... BUT I MAY ROTATE, GIVEN A GOOD SPIN...

I DON'T KNOW ABOUT YOU FOLKS, BUT THE LAST TIME I CHECKED, THE ENEMY OF MY ENEMY WAS MY FRIEND!
TEACH ON, GOLDILOCKS!

DOES IT THEN FOLLOW THAT THE FRIEND OF MY FRIEND IS MY ENEMY?
WHY, IT WOULD SEEM INDUBITABLY SO!

I SUPPOSE WE'D BEST KILL DORMOUSE THEN, WHILE WE'VE GOT HIM UNAWARES.

I PROPOSE THAT WE ALLY OURSELVES WITH BOOK-BURNER NOW. TODAY!
WE RALLY TO HIS CAUSE SO THAT WHEN HE EMERGES FROM THE FRAY VICTORIOUS, WE CAN TAKE OUR RIGHTFUL PLACES BY HIS SIDE!

AND WITH US ASSISTING HIM FROM WITHIN THE VERY WALLS THAT PROTECT THE MAN, VICTORY WILL! BE! HIS!
WHO'S WITH ME?!

HEY THERE, PRIS--UH, MISS PAGE, I MEAN.
WEIRD TIME TO BE HEADING OUT, ISN'T IT? CAN I SEE YOUR PAPERWORK?

LISTEN, JOE. YOU'VE HEARD ABOUT THE BOOKBURNER, RIGHT? YOU'VE HEARD HOW HE EATS HUMAN SKIN AND MAKES FURNITURE OUT OF BONES?
DO YOU WANT TO BE THE GUY WHO COSTS US THIS WAR BECAUSE YOU STOOD AROUND ASKING A BUNCH OF STUPID QUESTIONS?
UH...

DO YOU WANT TO SPEND THE REST OF YOUR SAD LITTLE CAREER PULLING NIGHTTIME DUTY, JOE? WOULDN'T YOU LIKE TO SEE THE SUN SOMEDAY?

OKAY, THORN. I GOT YOUR ASS OUT OF THE GOLDEN BOUGHS. SO, WHERE AM I TAKING YOU?
NEW YORK.

AND YOU MIGHT WANT TO HURRY, BECAUSE... WELL...
...ALL OF OUR LIVES MAY DEPEND ON IT.

NO, HILLARY WAS PRETTY SURE BY NOW THAT BOOKBURNER WAS NOT HER FATHER.
WELL, I IMAGINE THAT BY NOW OUR MUTUAL FRIEND MISTER D HAS SLAUGHTERED YOUR SISTER AND THAT HOOLIGAN, JACK OF THE TALES.
YOU THINK?
WHICH MADE THINGS EASIER, IN A WAY.
HEY, BURNER.
REMEMBER A LITTLE WHILE BACK--
--WHEN YOU ASKED ME WHAT HAPPENED TO THAT GIRL WHO KARATE-CHOPPED HER WAY OUT OF IDYLL?
YES?
SHE'S JUST BEEN WAITING FOR YOU TO GET LAZY.

HYAH!

YAH!
OOF!

OMAR!

I'VE HAD JUST ABOUT ENOUGH OF THIS POPPYCOCK.
GET THE KNIFEJOHNS AND MAKE SURE THAT SHE GETS TAKEN CARE OF!

WATCHING WALTER THE BALLROOM-DANCING UNICORN ON STAGE, YOU'D THINK THAT HE WAS ALL SWEETNESS AND LIGHT ON THE INSIDE, RIGHT?

WELL, YOU'D BE WRONG.
COME INSIDE THE CONDO AND YOU'LL SEE THE REAL WALTER. HE'S GOT LEATHER JACKETS AND GUNS AND KNIVES AND NUNCHUKS AND ALL SORTS OF TOUGH STUFF.

BUT THAT'S THE WAY IT IS--WHEN YOU GROW UP A UNICORN ON THE MEAN STREETS OF SOUTH PHILLY, YOU LEARN TO BE ROUGH--OR YOU DON'T MAKE IT OUT ALIVE.
LONG EYELASHES, RHINESTONE HORSESHOES, AND A FLUFFY PINK MANE MIGHT TAKE YOU PLACES IN SHOW BIZ, BUT IN THE GRITTY WORLD OF GANGS AND STREET THUGS, THEY MAKE YOU A TARGET.

BUT WITH A COMBINATION OF STREETWISE ATTITUDE AND A KILLER FOXTROT, WALTER KNEW HE COULD MAKE IT. HE JUST KNEW IT.
AND MAKE IT HE DID!

PFFF!

AND HEY, IF WALTER HAD TO TAKE OUT A FEW TALKING BUNNIES AND ELVES AND WHATNOT ALONG THE WAY--WELL, LIFE'S A BITCH, BABY!

I HAVE TO ADMIT I LIKE HILLARY BEST OF ALL. WANT TO KNOW WHY?
DAMMIT, RAVEN! DO SOME-THING!
ROBIN?
BECAUSE SHE FEELS EVERYTHING, AND SHE'S NOT AFRAID TO FEEL EVERYTHING.
ROBIN!!

AND SHE NEVER BACKS DOWN FROM A FIGHT.
MISTER D!

HANG ON, SIS!

HEY, HILLARY! LONG TIME NO SEE!

SHUT YOUR ***FACE,*** MAGGOT. I'M NOT HERE FOR YOU.

KNIFE-JOHNS ***WE,*** MANY AND MERRY.

COME TO CUT, AND ***CUT*** WE SHALL.

KNIFE-JOHNS ***ON!***

HEY, REMEMBER IN AMERICANA WHEN WE WERE ALL SURROUNDED BY INDIANS?

YEAH?

THIS IS KIND OF LIKE THAT, ONLY I'M ***PRETTY*** SURE WE'RE ALL ABOUT TO BE CUT TO RIBBONS.

SNIK

SNIK

SNIK

WELL, I DON'T KNOW ABOUT YOU, BUT I'D SAY THAT OUR HEROES ARE WELL AND TRULY HOSED, WOULDN'T YOU?
COME ON, THEN! I'VE FACED DOWN WORSE THAN YOU!
NOT LIKELY, THINK I.
I MEAN, THEY'RE OVERPOWERED, OUTMATCHED, COLD AND TIRED.
YOU KNOW WHAT WOULD BE GREAT? IF GARY WOULD WAKE THE HELL UP.
IT WOULDN'T DO ANY GOOD--HE DOESN'T LIKE HURT-ING PEOPLE.
NEWS FLASH, DUMBASS--I DON'T KNOW WHAT THEY ARE, BUT THESE GUYS AIN'T PEOPLE!
HONESTLY, I DON'T SEE HOW THEY'RE GETTING OUT OF THIS ONE.
HLK
EXCUSE ME. MAY I BE OF ASSISTANCE?

HEY, *LOOK*--
IT'S ME!
GOODNESS, WHAT A *PICKLE* WE FIND OURSELVES IN!
IT APPEARS I'VE SHOWED UP *JUST IN THE NICK OF TIME!* SPLENDID!

OH, GOSH! AS IT HAPPENED, THE KNIFEJOHNS ALL DEVELOPED A HORRIBLE CASE OF *INSTANT* PNEUMONIA AND DIED!
UNEX-PECTED!

HEY! LEMME UP, YOU YOUNG TURK!
WH...WHAT HAPPENED?

UH, GARY? YOU KNOW THIS GUY?
IT'S DEX. THE DEUS EX MACHINA.

HELLO, PATHETIC FALLACY.
OR SHOULD I CALL YOU "GARY" NOW?
GARY IS FINE, THANKS.

YOU HAD TO WAIT UNTIL THE VERY LAST MINUTE TO SHOW UP, DIDN'T YOU?
YOU'RE JUST A...A MEANIE!

WELL, I SEE YOU DO, IN FACT, REMEMBER ME.
VERY CONVENIENT, THAT MEMORY OF YOURS. YOU ALWAYS SEEM TO REGAIN IT AT EXACTLY THE MOMENT IT'S NEEDED.

KIND OF MAKES YOU WONDER, DOESN'T IT?

WELL, THAT'S THAT. MY WORK HERE IS DONE.
WE'LL JUST BE OFF.
BYE, ELIZA!
ROBIN!

COME ON, MISTER DEUS EX MACHINA--MAKE MY SISTER ALL BETTER!
SORRY, NO CAN DO, PET.

WHY THE HELL NOT? YOU MADE ALL THOSE MONSTERS DROP LIKE FLIES! SURELY YOU CAN HEAL HER!
SORRY, MY DEAR. I ONLY WORK EVERY ONCE IN A WHILE. AFTER THAT I GET OLD.
AND I'M TOO YOUNG TO GET OLD.

BUT...
I'M SO SORRY, HILLARY. I DID THE BEST I COULD.

COME ALONG, MISS WALL. LET'S FIND THOSE THREE BROTHERS OF YOURS AND GET A BITE TO EAT, SHALL WE?

SORRY, BUT THAT'S ALL I COULD DO. THERE'S A REASON NOBODY LIKES THE DEUS EX MACHINA, YOU KNOW.
AND SO IT BEGINS. BOOKBURNER'S ARMY ASSEMBLES.
FALL IN! PREPARE YOURSELVES, MY DREAD ***ARMY*** OF FORGOTTEN FABLES! ***PREPARE*** YOURSELVES!

HERE'S ***LITTLE LINDSAY LARIAT,*** "WHO ATE HER COAT AND THEN HER HAT."
REMEMBER HER? NO--OF COURSE YOU DON'T.

OR HOW ABOUT ***MAN O' FRUIT.*** HE MADE A SUIT OF PICKLED PEARS AND PLUMS.

AND PAUL BUNYAN, OF COURSE. THE MAN WHO ONCE TRAVELED THE ***LENGTH AND BREADTH*** OF AMERICANA WITH HIS TRUSTY BLUE OX AT HIS SIDE.
NO LONGER, SADLY.

AND ON AND ON THEY COME.
LINDY-LOU, THE PRAGMATIC CAT.
METZGER MOOSE (WITH HIS ASTONISHIN' JUICE).
AND WHAT OF OUR PAGE SISTERS? THE HEROINES OF THIS PIECE?
HERE'S HILLARY PAGE, TURNING TO A MAN SHE DETESTS FOR HELP IN HER DARKEST HOUR.
COME ON, JACK, HELP ME GET HER BACK TO THE GOLDEN BOUGHS. YOU OWE ME *THAT* MUCH, AT LEAST.
HERE'S ROBIN PAGE, TURNING PALE, FAR TOO MUCH OF HER BLOOD SEEPING INTO THE COLD GROUND.

THE COMANCHE SKELETON.
THE MYSTERIOUS HORNSWAGGLE.
YOU KNEW THEM ALL ONCE. AND NOW YOU'VE NEVER HEARD OF A SINGLE ONE.
AND THEY'RE COMING. ALL OF THEM.
AND HERE'S PRISCILLA PAGE, TURNING HER BACK ON THE MAN SHE'S FOLLOWED BLINDLY MOST OF HER LIFE.
I CAN'T BELIEVE I JUST... LEFT...WITHOUT PERMISSION!
OH, I IMAGINE YOU'LL PISS REVISE OFF A WHOLE LOT MORE BEFORE THIS IS ALL OVER.

DAMN IT ALL, SIS! WHO IN BLAZES ARE YOU TALKING TO? I DON'T SEE **ANY-ONE.**

OH, NEITHER DO I.

BUT IT'S ALWAYS **FUN** TO PRETEND, ISN'T IT?

*OKAY, THIS IS **OVER,** RIGHT? THERE'RE ONLY **THREE** PAGE SISTERS. AND I SHOULD KNOW BECAUSE I'VE HAD MY **OIL** CHANGED BY EACH AND EVERY ONE OF 'EM. THREE PAGE SISTERS, THREE ISSUES. THREE DOSES OF THAT BITCHY NARRATOR. **ENOUGH!** NEXT MONTH: THE SIEGE OF THE GOLDEN BOUGHS! AND NAKED CHICKS GALORE!*

BOLLAND

BOLLAND
OTEL
WELLS TANGO

HOT
BOLLAND

BOLLAND

BOLLAND
GOLDEN TREASURY OF
FAIRY TALES
The Sleeping Beauty
Arabian Nights
Rubaiyat Omar Khayyam